SKYSCRAPER SETTLEMENT

SKYSCRAPER SETTLEMENT

The Many Lives of Christodora House

JOYCE MILAMBILING

New Village Press • New York

Published in the United States by New Village Press
bookorders@newvillagepress.net
www.newvillagepress.org
New Village Press is a public-benefit, nonprofit publisher
Distributed by NYU Press
First Edition: September 2023

Paperback ISBN: 978-1-61332-215-4
Hardcover ISBN: 978-1-61332-216-1
eBook ISBN: 978-1-61332-217-8

Library of Congress Control Number: 2023940184

Front Cover Illustration: Lithograph of Christodora House by Diego Briceno
Back Cover Illustration: "Christodora House," oil painting by M. A. Tricca, 1934.
Courtesy of Smithsonian American Art Museum; Transfer from the U.S. Department of Labor.

In Memory of Leon A. Blanchette,
the most optimistic person I have ever known

CONTENTS

LIST OF ILLUSTRATIONS

The author and publisher would like to thank the institutions that have kindly given permission to reproduce these illustrations.

INTRODUCTION

From the Archives to Christodora House to the Streets of New York

AT MIDDAY IN LATE June 2017, I found a spot on a shaded bench in Tompkins Square Park, in New York City, and settled back to engage in some serious people watching. It was a Saturday afternoon in the city, and an assortment of adults and young people were walking, biking, and skateboarding past me. I also noticed some individuals standing along an interior fence in a line headed by a woman holding a clipboard. Taking a closer look, I saw that plates of food were being handed out when people reached the front of the line. A young man and woman along with their little boy joined me on the bench, and I asked who was distributing the meals. They told me these were being provided by a mission in the neighborhood.

I was not in that place by accident that day. Across the street on Avenue B, a few feet from one of the entrances to the park, is a sixteen-story brown brick building with a contrasting stone doorway decorated with bas-relief columns and ornate figures. The words *Christodora House* are etched in the light gray stone, along with the number 143, above the sturdy doors. From 1928 to 1948, this building was the site of the Christodora House social settlement, where college-educated residents, most of them women, taught classes and hosted clubs for the scores of immigrants who lived in crowded tenements in the surrounding neighborhood. Founded in 1897, Christodora House was always located in this neighborhood, and the building at 143 Avenue B was the latest, and grandest, locale. Constructed in 1928, it was called "the skyscraper settlement" because it towered over nearby buildings and was dedicated to settlement work on the first five stories and housed an associated "Club Residence" on the upper floors. This is a story of how an idea evolved, took physical shape, and adjusted not only to different physical locations but also to a changing neighborhood and city. As settlement houses carried the core values of the movement into the late twentieth century and then into the early twenty-first, Christodora House evolved and focused its energies on some of the vital strands of its work that have enabled it, retaining the name of Christodora, to continue to operate and thrive today.

Although the original settlement houses in the United States were founded on broad principles and spread a "Social Gospel" that did not usually proselytize for any one faith, the role that religion and religious ideology played in the settlement house movement was the subject of controversy then and remains so to this day. Christodora House, partly due to its name, which means "gift of Christ," was considered by some to be less secular than other settlement houses, despite its lack of formal ties with a specific religious sect. Christina MacColl, one of the founders of Christodora House, was adamant that their aim was not to convert their neighbors but, rather, "I believe it is thoroughly understood that our object is not to make Protestants out of Catholics or Christians out of Hebrews but to live out as best we know our lives and to help all with whom we come in contact to live at their best" (MacColl 1908).

Settlement house workers lived among the poor in the settlement house in order to bridge the considerable gap between the social classes by establishing connections with those who lived in the neighborhood and finding out what their needs were. Once the needs were determined, the settlement houses provided local children and families with classes, clinics, and other services that were not being supplied by the government or other agencies. In addition, many different kinds of clubs were formed for both children and adults, in which they could come together to explore common interests and learn about the environment around them. The immediate aim was to help immigrants settle more comfortably into their new lives, while the overarching goal was to establish a more just and equitable society. I was in the park that morning to acquire a sense of the place and historical era I had spent the previous year studying, and on which I have been working ever since.

My purpose is to tell the story of Christodora House, how it fit into the social conditions of New York City and community building on the Lower East Side, and how the organization and surrounding area have changed with the times. The "Many Lives" in the subtitle of this book refers to the scores of people whose lives Christodora House (and later, Christodora) have touched and the different locations at which the organization has carried out its work. The account begins with how a settlement house founded by two young women in 1897 developed and served its neighborhood during a time of dire need. The years after the Civil War had seen an increasing number of young women flocking to the cities to work, many of whom were new college graduates. Two of these individuals, Christina Mac-Coll and Sara Carson, founded the Young Women's Settlement on Avenue B, changing the name to Christodora House the following year. Other early settlement houses in New York City included University Settlement (originally called the Neighborhood Guild), founded in 1886; the College Settlement, established in 1889; and the Henry Street Settlement, which opened in 1893 under the name the Nurses' Settlement. There were settlement houses in other U.S cities, not only on the East Coast but also in other parts of the country, and by 1910 there were more than four hundred settlement houses across the country (Hansan 2011).

An important part of this narrative is also how the building at 143 Avenue B, home of the sixteen-story Christodora House settlement from 1928 to 1948, has represented different things to different people. Christodora House faces Tompkins Square Park, a public park that has been the backdrop for numerous political, social, and cultural movements and upheavals over the years, some of which have directly involved Christodora House. The building at 143 Avenue B housed a settlement house that had already been operating in physical locations other than the "skyscraper settlement" structure since 1897, and it continued its operations after 1948 at other sites. Christodora House always had a clear and consistent mission—namely, to bridge the social gap between the residents of the neighborhood and individuals who were qualified to offer educational, health, and other services. What the building symbolized changed over time; at first, it was a haven for its neighbors in an overcrowded city beset by problems and home to "settlers" who worked with local families, and then it was an example of a building acquired by the government under the doctrine of eminent domain. With time, the structure at 143 Avenue B suffered from neglect and contributed to the outward signs of urban decay in the area. Decades later, the building became a symbol of neighborhood gentrification when it was converted into condominiums. Finally, the building was recognized for its historical significance and was added to the State Register and the National Register of Historic Places in 1986.

TREASURES IN THE ARCHIVES

The idea for this book began when I was researching personal accounts of immigrants learning English in New York City at different periods of history. In the process, I discovered an electronic catalog listing of a collection of letters that was part of the holdings of the Patricia Klingenstein Library at the New-York Historical Society (NYHS) (Helen Schechter Letters, 1918). The thirty-three handwritten letters were written over the course of 1918 by a young immigrant widow named Helen Schechter to Ellen Gould, a woman who taught English classes at the local settlement house. The letters were housed in the society's archives and not available online, so I began a correspondence with the NYHS library staff and obtained photocopies of a limited number of these letters.

Over the next few months, I received two more batches of copies of the letters, and the story of Helen Schechter slowly began to take shape. The missives chronicle her dreams and frustrations as she raises four children in a teeming city beset with the problems endemic to rapid urbanization and industrialization. It was, nonetheless, a place she had come to love. The recipient of the letters, Ellen Gould, was a volunteer from Minnesota who taught English at Christodora House. The letters speak volumes about Helen Schechter's life and that of her children as she talks about daily events, including the family's involvement with activities at the settlement house located just down the street from their apartment on Avenue B.

As facts began to emerge from the letters about Helen Schechter and her ties with Christodora House, questions started arising about the circumstances surrounding the correspondence and about the addressee, Ellen Gould. As I was learning more about Helen Schechter in the letters, I realized that there were only sparse details about her life and that of her teacher within the letters themselves. It became clear that I would need to fill in much of the context, but only some of that research could be done at a distance. I traveled to New York to examine the letters in person and to find out more about these women and the neighborhood, both of which were starting to become real to me.

Archives are repositories of public records or historical materials such as documents and photographs and are commonly established by an organization to keep material that is important to it and relevant to its purpose. The NYHS archives encompass an extensive and varied collection of original manuscripts and other material, much of which has yet to be made available online. The mission of the NYHS, founded in 1804, is to offer visitors "on-site and online a vast collection of art, objects, artifacts, and documents, and an ongoing collecting program that aims to facilitate a broad grasp of history's enduring importance and its usefulness in finding explanations, causes, and insights" (New-York Historical Society).

I have visited the library at the NYHS, on the Upper West Side of Manhattan, a number of times now. The archives of that library are like many others where objects from the past are just waiting to be investigated: "We go to the archives not to find answers, but to articulate a better set of questions" (King 2011, 20). While conducting archival research within the library walls, I sat near scholars who were studying a wide variety of material: Some of them were poring over blueprints or maps spread out in front of them, while others wore gloves and were closely examining books or handwritten texts held in special holders, called "cradles." Researchers there on any one day are investigating different periods in the history of the city, ranging from hundreds of years ago to the present day.

I once attended a lecture by historian Stanley Katz in which he extolled the value of primary sources in research and teaching. He told the audience that at his university he had stopped using textbooks; instead, his students explored original source material under his guidance. His words came back to me the first time I opened the plain manila folder containing the set of handwritten letters written by Helen Schechter some one hundred years ago. Most of them were on small sheets of lined notebook paper, while others had been penned on fragile cream-colored stationery decorated with orange flowers. I was grateful for the opportunity to examine these letters in their original form firsthand, but I gradually came to realize that the content of these pages told only a small part of a much larger story. As I delved further into the Schechter letters, I became aware that to truly understand what she wrote, I first needed to find out more about the world and circumstances in which she and her family had lived.

Shortly before my first research trip to New York, I found out that a large collection of Christodora House records was housed in the Rare Book and Manuscript Library of Columbia University. This expanded, exponentially, the number of original sources available to me. The valuable records and documents that have been painstakingly saved and cataloged there are essential if one is to understand the purpose and significance of Christodora House at the time of its founding, as well as its development over time. During several research trips to the library, I systematically examined myriad typed and handwritten documents, including letters, annual reports, and minutes of club meetings. The collection also includes a large number of photographs and scrapbooks. These materials helped me to better understand the purpose of Christodora House, what its workers and donors provided in terms of services and events, and the profound significance that the building and staff held for the people of the neighborhood and for New York City. Particularly touching were the many letters I found in the library from Christina MacColl and other staff to and from the donors and friends of Christodora House, some of whom I recognized as well-known philanthropists. Most of the letter writers, however, were everyday people who expressed appreciation or donated money or material on their own as individuals or as a part of a family, or on behalf of their respective businesses, nonprofits, or other types of organizations.

THE SETTLEMENT HOUSE IN THE URBAN LANDSCAPE

During the course of my research, I have collected a great deal of information and have encountered a wide range of views about urban politics, the settlement house, and other social movements. This was complemented by published descriptions of the work and evolution of Christodora and other settlement houses. Contained within these original and secondary sources was a wide range of facts, opinions, and claims. In the process, I expanded my inquiry to include the late 1800s and the U.S. historical period known as the Progressive Era, from approximately 1900 to 1920.

The period between the mid-nineteenth century and early twentieth century was a time of tremendous growth in New York and other U.S. cities, but this came at a cost. Newcomers arrived in an environment completely alien to them, and they often faced extremely difficult living conditions. Migration to the cities from abroad as well as by single women and Black and white workers from the southern United States profoundly impacted social conditions and the demographics of the country. A wide variety of languages, cultures, and religions were characteristic of New York City and, more specifically, of the Lower East Side. Poverty, sweatshops, child labor, and inadequate sanitation were only a few of the realities faced by those who lived and worked on the historical Lower East Side.

In response to the conditions at that time, a number of voluntary associations arose in the absence of governmental intervention. One of the central themes explored in this book is how, when witnessing people who were living under the most difficult of circumstances, some individuals and groups did not stand idly by but, rather, marshaled their resources and gathered others to provide aid, encouragement, and, ultimately, hope. The motivations of those who headed and worked in settlement houses and other philanthropic organizations varied and have been subject to considerable analysis and criticism, some of which will be examined here. Nonetheless, the collective efforts of settlement house workers and other like-minded groups provided vital monetary and other forms of assistance to people in need at a point in history when cities were rapidly expanding and changing. Important questions arose and are still being asked about how much of this was done in the name of assimilating the newcomers or to convert them to Christianity (in particular Protestantism), and to what extent the home cultures and deep-seated values of the migrants were taken into consideration in the process.

The settlement house was one mechanism by which inhabitants of some of the poorest neighborhoods in Manhattan were able to receive educational, health, and other important services. These buildings were home to settlers whose own lives had been relatively privileged, and each settlement house was a home that was open to the neighbors for classes, clubs, lectures, and health and other services. Those who moved to the cities to live in the settlement houses came to do their part to help improve the lives of those who lived under conditions that they themselves had never experienced. These settlers, often female and newly graduated from college, lived in the settlement houses for different periods of time, in some cases for years. By residing in parts of the city where access to services was limited or nonexistent, the inhabitants of the settlement houses were able to form relationships, became part of the local community, and, as a result, played a role in bringing about social change in an era that desperately needed it.

CHRISTODORA HOUSE: THE BUILDING, THE ORGANIZATION, AND THE NEIGHBORHOOD

The building constructed in 1928 at 143 Avenue B that housed the Christodora House settlement has had a complex and often controversial history. After the settlement house at that location could no longer afford to operate there, the city of New York took over the building (with "just compensation" paid to Christodora House), after which the building gradually fell into disrepair. It changed hands several times and in the 1980s underwent extensive renovation and was converted into condominiums, sparking violent protests over the ongoing gentrification of the neighborhood. The Christodora settlement house carried on its work, however, and the building known as the "skyscraper settlement" was only one of several locales where its workers provided educational, recreational, and health services for people in the neighborhood.

Although the public service that Christodora House was known for is no longer the building's purpose, Christodora still exists today in the form of a nonprofit foundation known simply as Christodora, with an office on East Fifty-third Street. Christodora has continued to carry on the tradition of serving the community, now more broadly conceived, in ways that suit the present time. In the spirit of Northover Camp, which in its time was a summer haven for children and families who came to Christodora House, the nonsectarian Christodora Inc. emphasizes nature, education, and leadership. "What began as a settlement house in 1897 is now an 'ecosystem' of programs providing support and learning for middle and high school students—in public school classrooms, in natural areas around the city, and at our camp and other wilderness sites around the country" (Christodora Inc.). This emphasis on the natural world and our connection to it echoes the work and activities that had taken place through Christodora House's field trips and summer camp. For many years, Christodora has conducted youth programs and summer camps in New York City and New Jersey, and, since 1981, at the Manice Education Center in the Berkshire Hills.

The Christodora House structure, including its transformation over time, is in many ways a microcosm of New York City and the people who have shaped it. The East Village, the Lower East Side, and the Tompkins Square Park area have changed significantly over the years, but a sizable number of its residents still face poverty, health disparities, and homelessness. The fact that food was being distributed in Tompkins Square Park during my 2017 visit by a charitable organization was a reminder that, well into the twenty-first century, there are still inhabitants in the city who are struggling. The onset of COVID-19 a few years later only worsened that state of affairs.

The vital neighborhood that is the East Village has endured and continues to engage in new forms of community building and strengthening. Today, the East Village Community Coalition (EVCC) occupies space in Christodora House and is committed to supporting local residents and preserving the character and vibrancy of that neighborhood and community. Recent neighborhood and local activism, including efforts to help residents recover from the COVID-19 pandemic, further illustrate the ways in which care for one another, resistance, and resilience, qualities that have long characterized this part of the city, live on.

THE LEGACY OF THE SETTLEMENT HOUSE

The type of social service provider that was the settlement house filled a genuine need at a particular point in history. Over time, some of the individual houses and organizations evolved, while others eventually ceased to exist. It is a testament to the nature of settlement houses that they launched the careers of many individuals who influenced a number of other social movements and had a lasting effect on local and federal legislation. Julia Lathrop, the first woman to head a U.S. federal agency, the Children's Bureau, was a resident of Hull House in Chicago for two decades and was one of the authors of a groundbreaking study that documented the conditions under which immigrants lived in the late nineteenth century. Harry Hopkins was initiated into the world of social work at Christodora's summer camp in New Jersey and then continued to work at Christodora's Manhattan location. Hopkins led a life of public service and has been credited with helping to shape the sweeping domestic reforms known as the New Deal, enacted by President Franklin D. Roosevelt in the 1930s.

The settlement house as an institution provided a blueprint for how professions such as social work and nursing were to be carried out, especially in urban areas that contained significant immigrant and/or low-income populations. Robert Woods, Graham Taylor, and Lillian Wald are examples of settlement house leaders whose social outreach and activities were at the cutting edge of emerging professions and social movements. Other head workers of settlement houses, such as Christina MacColl of Christodora House and Helena Dudley of Denison House, were not as well known, but they nonetheless had a lasting effect on scores of immigrants who learned English, participated in clubs, and were afforded the opportunity to learn a trade. Settlement houses were not only physical buildings but also, in a metaphorical sense, functioned as "cooperative structures" that relied on the labor and determination of the resident workers and other staff as well as the participation and enthusiasm of the neighbors in the areas where the houses were located.

One lesser-known contribution of settlement houses was their involvement in and influence on art and culture. Christodora House's Poets' Guild, established by Anna Hempstead Branch, consisted of a distinguished group of authors who brought poetry and literature directly into the neighborhood. It was not unusual for settlement houses in New York and other metropolitan areas to serve as locales for artistic expression and to remain essential to their cities' arts communities for decades to come. The Third Street Music School Settlement on East Eleventh Street, founded in 1894 by Emilie Wagner, is a prime example of the influence of settlement houses on the arts and is the longest-running community music school in the United States.

CHAPTER OVERVIEWS

In addition to the introduction and conclusion, this book is divided into three parts, each consisting of three chapters. In the first chapter, historical background information is provided that describes the process by which migrants, from both within and outside the United States, entered and transformed the cities that received them. The newcomers were also changed as they adapted to the conditions of their lives, particularly in the period after the Civil War and into the twentieth century, a time of rapid industrialization and a changing economy. The focus is on New York City and the Lower East Side during a time when men and women from vastly different backgrounds came together and built new lives despite societal pressures and inequities caused by racism, xenophobia, and gender bias.

Chapter 2 describes how, alarmed by growing social and economic disparities in the United States, a wide range of individuals called for action. Together with some of the same people who were responsible for the situation, they formed an unlikely alliance that worked toward solving the most pressing issues facing the country. The third and final chapter in this part describes and analyzes the social settlement movement, starting with Toynbee Hall, in England, and continuing with settlement houses in the United States, exploring how those who worked in the latter adjusted the English model to fit markedly different conditions. Some of the New World settlement houses and their leaders became well known nationally and internationally, while others were less in the public eye but had a profound impact on their communities, nonetheless.

The second part of this book focuses on the Christodora settlement house and the environment in which it operated, starting in 1897. Two young women recognized in the settlement house movement a social structure that would enable them to live where they could serve their neighbors while bridging the gap between the middle class and the poor. An important distinction is made in this section between the work in which

Christodora House engaged and the different places in which its workers labored. The settlement house was located in two separate buildings on Avenue B until 1948, and starting in the early 1900s, children and families were also given the opportunity to spend time at Northover, Christodora's rural summer camp in New Jersey. In 1948, while still operating the camp, Christodora House moved from Avenue B and thereafter was based in a public housing project and in other buildings in the area. Finally, Christodora lives on in its present form, working with urban youth in New York City, guiding them in their development of academic self-efficacy and the skills they need to interact effectively and harmoniously with the human and natural worlds. The organization continues to work with an underserved population, and its reach has extended beyond Manhattan to other New York City boroughs.

In the third and final part of the book, I stand back and look at the settlement house and the communities in which it operated from the perspective of today. Chapter 7 examines some of the controversies and claims regarding the settlement house movement as well as ways in which the institution and people who worked within it were a product of their time. What were some of the underlying motives and objectives of the settlement house movement, and what are some of the criticisms that have been leveled at the movement in the past and up until now?

How settlement houses have adapted to changing populations and methods of delivering social services is explored in chapter 8. The impact and legacy of the settlement house movement is examined, as well as, for those settlement houses that have survived, what was retained and what changed. Even though settlement workers no longer live in today's settlement houses and community centers, the people who work in those institutions oftentimes live in the neighborhood. The present conception of the settlement house mirrors the earlier model but now places an emphasis on community strengths rather than deficits: A settlement house is a "neighborhood-based social organization that provides services designed to identify and reinforce the strengths of individuals, families, and communities" (United Neighborhood Houses of New York). As in the past, the programs offered at each settlement house reflect the needs of its particular neighborhood and those who live there.

The final chapter of this part of the book defines and looks at community building and social advocacy in the East Village and Lower East Side. The focus is on the East Village over the decades and how a neighborhood of creative, resilient individuals and groups of people have worked not only to survive but to thrive. I will also look at obstacles that have stood in the way of creating and sustaining this vibrant community and how a variety of social service organizations, including but not limited to settlement houses, have met the varied challenges they have faced.

Viewing the settlement house movement from the perspective of subjects like immigration, religion, poverty, and social justice is bound to result in different and often conflicting interpretations of people and events. As Fisher and Fabricant (2002) observed, "Historians and social work academicians interested in social welfare history have written widely on the settlement house, each with a different lens, asking different questions, looking at different settlements, and often arriving at different conclusions" (3). Taken together, these varied accounts can serve to deepen our knowledge of the settlement house movement and help us gain a more balanced understanding of the individuals who inspired and sustained it.

By examining the wealth of historical records and studying the settlement house movement, I came to realize how vital it is to give voice to the people responsible for creating a place like Christodora House. They forged relationships across social classes and ensured that vital facilities and services were available to the neighborhood decade after decade, all without much fanfare or recognition. It is especially important to highlight the contributions of the women at Christodora House like Margaret Widdemer and Anna Hempstead Branch, as well as to examine how the settlement house staff and board members persevered during the years in which the organization operated out of temporary quarters and struggled to stay afloat financially. All the while, they kept their work relevant to the times and to those they served.

Another goal in focusing on the settlement house movement and presenting this account of Christodora House is to provide some clarity on the motivations and accomplishments of the settlements' founders, settlers, donors, and neighbors, many of whom are unfamiliar to the reader of today. After all, what those individuals achieved and what their intentions were have become blurred with time and have been subject to wide-ranging interpretation. However, a significant record remains in the form of their words and the words of those who were impacted by their endeavors. There are also policies and laws, such as those regulating child labor and sanitation, that settlement house workers were instrumental in enacting, even though the settlement leaders and staff are not always given credit for their accomplishments in history books. A quote that was part of an exhibit at the New-York Historical Society about the history of public monuments is equally relevant to the settlement house movement: "History is not truth; it's memory, and a part of remembering is considering what we forgot" (Johnson 2010, para.4).

Figure I.1. New York City Views. View northwest from the roof of the Christodora House. Photo February 5, 1929, by Samuel H. Gottscho (1875–1971), Museum of the City of New York.

PART I

THE HISTORICAL SETTING

I

MIGRATION AND URBAN TRANSFORMATION

Migration: The movement of persons away from their place of usual residence, either across an international border or within a State.

See also circular migration, climate migration, displacement, economic migration, facilitated migration, family migration, forced migration, human mobility, internal migration, international migration, irregular migration, labor migration, migrant, mixed migration, safe, orderly and regular migration, resettlement, return migration.

—Alice Sironi, Céline Bauloz, and Milen Emmanuel, eds.,
"International Migration Law: Glossary on Migration."

ECONOMIC GROWTH AND DOWNTURNS, natural disasters, famine, climate change, and war are only some of the drivers of international migration. Currently, due to political upheaval and violence taking place worldwide, refugees and other migrants are flocking to countries where they can live safely and, if necessary, build new lives. As a result, migrants can be found in North America and in all corners of the world. Some of these migrants become long-term immigrants in the countries to which they travel, while others do not.

John F. Kennedy's declaration "We are a nation of immigrants" has long been used as a slogan by individuals and groups who have championed and continue to promote the cause and status of immigrants to the United States.[1] As crucial as the immigrants who arrived from Europe and other continents have been and continue to be for the building and prosperity of the country, it is fundamentally inaccurate to maintain that the United States is a nation solely of immigrants. "The often idealized American immigrant story that involves invoking the elusive 'American dream' typically leaves out Black and Indigenous experiences in ways that fail to build bridges amid and across different experiences of marginalization" (Cohen 2020). In an account of who has populated the United States and how different groups have been characterized at different points in history, Dunbar-Ortiz (2021) states, "The claim that the United States is 'a nation of immigrants' is the benevolent version of U.S. nationalism. The ugly, predominant side is the panic of enemy invasion" (279). The lives and experiences not only of immigrants but also of Indigenous peoples, slaves, and their descendants need to be acknowledged as an integral piece of the collective history of this nation. Furthermore, it is crucial that the harm done to those who are still seen and treated as "other," and therefore dangerous, be condemned by all sectors of society.

The initial focus in this chapter is on those who migrated to U.S. cities during the late 1800s and early 1900s. People came from all over the world for a multitude of reasons, many of them remaining in the cities where they first stepped foot in the country. This is complemented by an account of the "migration from within" that features the women and men who did not cross any national borders but, rather, were flocking to urban areas within the United States in search of greater opportunities, including but not limited to economic ones. Much of what is described here refers to New York and the area known historically as the Lower East Side, the area in which Christodora House is located and where its settlement house workers lived among their neighbors. In addition to indicating geographic location, place names such as the Five Points, the Lower East Side, Greenwich Village, the East Village, Alphabet City, Loisaida, Little Italy, and Chinatown, among others, have functioned as markers of both belonging and leaving behind, solidarity and exclusivity.

The chapter continues with an overview of the adverse conditions that were common in the tenement buildings, alleyways, and streets of the Lower East Side during the latter half of the nineteenth century and into the twentieth. These unsafe and unhealthy housing and work environments were increasingly revealed to the public by a succession of journalists, social and health workers, politicians who were not part of the infamous "machines," and political activists. The words, images, and actions of these individuals and groups raised awareness of how "the other half lives" and how this was connected to rapid industrialization and the unequal distribution of wealth in the United States. The efforts of activists and journalists (some of whom were famously called "muckrakers") paved the way for vital organizations and social movements that sought to remedy the most pressing problems of the day. The ultimate goal was to transform the city so that it would become more livable for everyone.

IMMIGRATION: FACTS AND CONSEQUENCES

Immigrants from a wide variety of countries have long had different motivations for settling in what is now the United States.

Newcomers from Northern and Western Europe, including Scandinavia and the British Isles, had been common in early waves, starting in colonial times. They sought a greater potential for working, owning land, and feeding their families than was available in their home countries. Significant waves of immigration to the United States occurred during the colonial era, the first part of the nineteenth century, and from the 1880s to 1920. Between 1815 and 1845, it has been estimated that one million people from Ireland alone had immigrated to America. This number increased when Irish migrants sought to escape the Great Famine of 1845 and the harsh policies of British rule.

The steady pace of industrialization, which intensified after the Civil War ended in 1865, had attracted masses of immigrants to U.S. cities and towns. It has been estimated that over 300,000 Chinese workers (mostly male) had already immigrated to this country as a result of the Gold Rush (1848–1852) and continued to arrive during the three decades between 1852 and 1882 to meet the demand for manual laborers. Due to anti-Asian violence in the western states starting in the 1870s, scores of Chinese workers migrated eastward to other parts of the country. The Chinese Exclusion Act took effect in 1882 and Chinese immigration to the United States was officially suspended for a period of ten years. Migrants originally from China who already resided in the United States, along with some who managed to enter despite the ban, formed new communities or expanded existing ones. In the process, they adapted to their circumstances despite rampant discrimination. "By the turn of the [twentieth] century, Chinese could be found in every state of the union. They worked where they could, usually in agriculture, domestic service, restaurants, or laundries, and they clustered in Chinatown communities that sprang up in many towns to serve their social, economic, and political needs" (Yung, Chang, and Lai 2006, 4).

Italians were another group that figured prominently in major migrations to this country. At the end of the nineteenth century in Italy, crippling taxation, chronic disease, and crop failure had forced large numbers of these Southern Europeans from their native land. They migrated to different parts of Europe and to North and South America, Argentina in particular. Many of these migrants returned to Italy or made several trips back and forth, and it was not until 1900 that more Italians immigrated to the United States than to South America. It is estimated that between 1901 and 1914, more than three million Italians immigrated to the United States (Wallace 2017, 194).

Many of the immigrants who arrived in New York City during the early twentieth century came from some of the same places they do today: "The metropolis embraced massive migration from southern and eastern Europe, along with smaller inflows from northern Europe, the Middle and Far East, the Caribbean and Central/South America" (Wallace 2017, 8). In addition to Italy, sizable numbers of European immigrants came from Greece, the Balkan region, and areas of Eastern Europe under the control of Prussia, the Austro-Hungarian Empire, and Russia.[2] Many immigrants who entered through the port of New York remained in the city and settled in neighborhoods in Manhattan and the outer boroughs. Other immigrants continued on to a wide range of cities and rural areas in other parts of the United States.

By the mid-nineteenth century in Manhattan, there was already a well-established German-speaking community called Kleindeutschland ("Little Germany") within the area that would later be called the Lower East Side. Consisting of both Jews and non-Jews, these Germans were highly skilled workers, such as mechanics and carpenters. Other early German immigrants specialized in occupations such as shoemaking, brewing, and furniture making. By 1880, "German Jews started to abandon the quarter and, in their drive toward Americanization and respectability, moved uptown" (Maffi 1995, 117). At the end of the nineteenth century and into the twentieth, there was a major influx of Jewish immigrants from Central and Eastern Europe who emigrated from their homelands and settled in the United States, especially in New York City.

Laws in the 1880s in the Russian Empire and other parts of Eastern Europe restricted where Jews could live and how they could earn a living, thus forcing many to emigrate, very often with their whole families. "The largest tributary flowed out of tsarist Russia, with over 1.5 million Jews leaving for America between 1881 and 1914, including Lithuanian (from Lithuania and Belorussia), Polish, Bessarabian, and Ukrainian Jews" (Soyer 1997, 27). Many were escaping anti-Semitism and the threat of targeted massacres known as pogroms. The influx of Eastern European Jews who settled on the Lower East side led to a distinction being made between the "uptown Jews" who had moved from the area and those who had arrived more recently and were dismissively referred to as the "downtown Jews."

An Ambivalent Welcome

One way to characterize how immigrants were viewed by those already in residence is in positive terms: "The 'generous heart of America' welcomed more than 17 million immigrants to the United States from the day the Statue of Liberty was dedicated in 1886 to the beginning of World War I, twenty-eight years later—a movement of people without precedent in human history" (Anbinder 2016, 327). The reality of how they were received, however, was more complex. Theodore Roosevelt, the twenty-sixth president of the United States, who was in office from 1901 to 1909, played an important role in how immigration and immigrants were viewed and talked about at the turn of the twentieth century and into the twenty-first. In the face of this, Roosevelt attempted to keep to a middle ground and he "opted to neither offer unmitigated praise of immigrants nor take a nativist stance. Instead, Roosevelt's rhetoric reveals his struggle to carefully distinguish 'immigration of the right kind' from that 'of the wrong kind,' as he put it in his third annual message to Congress" (Childers 2015, 185).

Not all of the immigrants who intended to live in the United States for the long term had the legal right to become citizens through the process of naturalization. Starting in 1790, when the first naturalization law was enacted by Congress, all "free white persons" who had resided in the country for two years, were of "good moral character," and were ready to swear allegiance to the Constitution were eligible for naturalization. (Foreign-born women were only able to receive citizenship through their husbands until the law was revised in 1922 to include married and unmarried females.) A number of other revisions to naturalization law, including automatic citizenship for children born in the country, eligibility for naturalization for those of African birth, and exclusion of Chinese nationals from naturalization, were made over the years (Desipio and DeGarza 2015).

The revised Naturalization Act of 1906, which added the requirement that immigrants needed to be able to learn English in order to become naturalized citizens, was supported and signed into law by President Theodore Roosevelt. The enduring themes of acceptance and assimilation as well as who were the

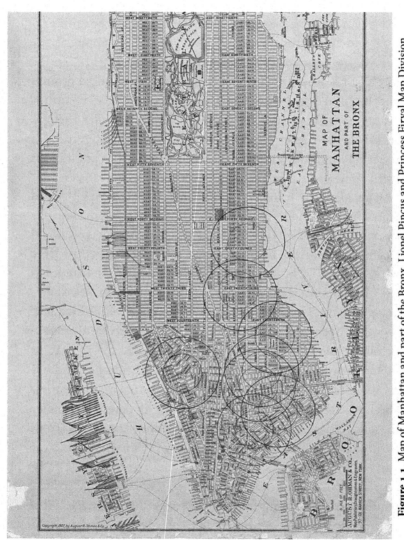

Figure 1.1. Map of Manhattan and part of the Bronx. Lionel Pincus and Princess Firyal Map Division, New York Public Library Digital Collections.

"right" and the "wrong" sort of immigrants and therefore worthy to stay permanently are vital to an analysis of assimilation efforts, the transformation of U.S. cities, and of past and present politics and policies.

Immigrants and the Lower East Side

Neighborhoods on the island of Manhattan have long been in flux, both in terms of what the different areas have been referred to as well as who has resided there. Anbinder (2016) identified the Jewish weekly publication *The Jewish Messenger* as first using the moniker "Lower East Side" in 1880, but the author also noted that it took several more years before the name was widely used to refer to that part of Manhattan. "Comprising more than 250 square blocks, the Lower East Side was far too big to be called a neighborhood; it was really a series of neighborhoods" (Anbinder 2016, 356–57).

This fluidity of borders and the changing names for various areas have been commonplace tendencies throughout the history of the island of Manhattan. In the case of the Lower East Side and other parts of Lower Manhattan, immigrants lived where they could find work and affordable housing. They tended to cluster in the blocks and neighborhoods where compatriots or people who spoke the same language could be found. Prior to 1880, there were African Americans, Irish men and women, Germans, Hungarians, and Ukrainians, along with a small group of Chinese immigrants, among others, who lived in different pockets of the southern part of the island. The Five Points was an area half a mile northeast of the present-day City Hall, where several streets converged, and in the mid-nineteenth century this area was home to large numbers of immigrants, especially German and Irish. "The neighborhood became lodged in collective memory as a place of crime, prostitution and disorder, but it primarily served as a home and workplace for a struggling but burgeoning working-class population" (Polland and Soyer 2012, 19). It was a place where the poorest of residents, particularly Irish Catholics and African Americans, were at the mercy of absentee landlords and escalating crime. Jobs in the shipyards and ports had initially drawn large numbers of workers to the Five Points, along with the establishments that served them. By 1854, the maritime industry in the city was dwindling, and "U.S. cities changed from mercantile to industrial functions" (Lin 1994, 47).

In addition to economic shifts, diversity and changes in who lived in the area were constantly making and remaking the Lower East Side. In the first two decades of the twentieth century, the Lower East Side contained some distinctive enclaves of immigrants, but there was also a mix of those who belonged to a wide range of ethnicities and religions on individual streets and in the same neighborhoods. In addition to the large numbers of Jewish immigrants from Eastern Europe, members of many other nationalities, ethnicities, and religious affiliations settled there as well. A map produced in 1919 by John Trevor, whose title was given as "Special Deputy Attorney for the Joint Legislative Committee Investigating Seditious Activities," showed that the Lower East Side contained large concentrations of Russian Jews, Italians, Austro-Hungarians, Italians, and a somewhat smaller area with what remained of the original German population. Substantial numbers of Irish and Italian immigrants had also formed their own neighborhoods farther west, but still below Fourteenth Street (Wallace 2017, 1031–34). On the same map, the area bordering Tomkins Square Park, the part of the Lower East Side that was served by Christodora House, was labeled as "mixed."

In the collective memory of American Jews, the Lower East Side is often thought of with nostalgia as the place where many of their ancestors started their lives in *di goldene medina* ("the golden land"). The community of tenement buildings and push-carts "provided the stage for immigrants' first encounter with American daily life, a remarkably consistent stage over the twenty-five blocks of Manhattan's Lower East Side, where three hundred thousand Jews lived by 1893" (Polland and Soyer 2012, 113). There is a rich literature concerning the Jewish presence on the Lower East Side, as well as a number of documentaries and other types of films. In addition to Polland and Soyer's vol-ume on New York Jews between 1840 and 1920, detailed accounts of Jewish life in previous centuries in the United States can be found in sources such as Klapper (2005), Moore et al. (2017), and Soyer (1997), among many others.

United Hebrew Charities and Beth Israel Hospital were among the organizations created to support the Jewish commu-nity in New York. There were also many associations established by and for immigrants who came from the same hometowns or areas. One example of a type of association that catered to the Jewish population was the landsmanshaft. "Thrown together in the congested immigrant neighborhoods of the New World, it is not surprising that they retained a strong sense of identifi-cation with their native towns" (Soyer 1997, 27). In addition to the personal ties that the landsmanshaft helped strengthen, many of them also provided assistance that was either not available or not affordable, such as help with obtaining life insurance and finding housing.

A Jewish organization that is lesser known today was the Industrial Removal Office (IRO), which operated from 1901 to 1922. Originally part of the Jewish Agricultural Society, this office was established by German American Jews to relocate unemployed Jewish (mostly Eastern European) residents from New York and other East Coast cities to states farther west that were less densely populated. They were placed in a wide range of occupations and trades, and among their ranks were carpenters, butchers, blacksmiths, printers, and weavers. The organization had specific goals that balanced the needs of the immigrants with those of the places to which they relocated: "Distribution represented neither an end in itself nor a wholesale scheme to relocate under any circumstance New York's unemployed immigrant Jews. Rather it would make possible the self-support thousands could not achieve in New York, which was a single crucial step pointing the way toward a new, responsible life in the United States" (Glazier 2006, 19–20). The efforts of the IRO were part of a broader strategy to assimilate and Americanize the newcomers and eventually resulted in the resettlement of approximately 79,000 people to towns and cities throughout the United States and Canada (Center for Jewish History). However well meaning the intentions of those operating the IRO might have been (and this is debatable), not all Jews who were deemed candidates for relocation welcomed such a drastic move away from their current neighborhood, and not all of the receiving communities were anxious to welcome them.

New York City was for many years a hub for the garment industry. This required a veritable army of workers, some of whom were employed in factories, while other laborers worked on the materials in their homes. An account of the history of the Lower East Side would not be complete without mention of those contractors or middlemen whom Jacob Riis, in his book *How the Other Half Lives* (1890), referred to as "the sweaters." To understand who these individuals were, it is necessary to understand how the garment industry operated at the time: "The term 'sweatshop' applied not because of the heat but rather the manner in which manufacturers 'sweated' profit from contractors, who in turn sweated profit from laborers" (Polland and Soyer 2012, 120). The sweatshops and those who benefited from them were motivated by profit, and the human toll was heartbreaking. Men, women, and even children assembled items like clothing and artificial flowers with materials supplied by manufacturers. Often laboring in their cramped living quarters, they were paid a pittance for their work and were required to turn out huge piles of clothing each week just to make ends meet. Legislation that regulated some aspects of this so-called home work was eventually passed in New York and elsewhere, but the practice continued, both legally and illegally.

Advances in machinery and expansion of facilities did not entirely eliminate the sweatshop system in the garment industry: "Manufacturers could incorporate sweating procedures by turning over inside space to outside contractors and leaving them to hire the machine operators, usually young immigrant girls; competition between such 'inside contractors' could be counted on to force wages down" (Wallace 2017, 319). The immigrants who worked in the tenement sweatshops as well as the factory-based ones were largely Jewish and Italian, a fact that would be demonstrated when the ethnicities of those who died in the devastating Triangle Shirtwaist Factory Fire of 1911 were identified (Giunta and Trasciatti 2022).

MIGRATION FROM WITHIN

It was not only immigrants from other countries who flooded into U.S. cities at the turn of the twentieth century and in the first few decades of the twenty-first. They were joined by migrants from small towns and rural areas within the United States, particularly from the South. Laws enacted restricting immigration into this country had intensified the need for workers: "Between 1870 and 1921, Congress passed 20 pieces of legislation restricting immigration. When measures aimed at controlling the origins of immigrants failed to work, Congress imposed a numerical limit with the Quota Law of 1921" (Spain 2001, 40). Some of the large numbers of migrants originally from other places within the United States came to work in the steel mills, railroads, and factories, while others sought work in homes and offices in the burgeoning metropolises. These newcomers put additional strain on the already inadequate infrastructure in many cities.

The phrase "migration from within" refers to the movement of migrants from other cities, towns, and rural areas within the United States to cities, primarily those in the Northeast, from the late 1800s until about 1930. There is a particular focus in historical accounts of this internal migration on those who relocated from the largely rural South to the urban North in that time period, even though migrants continued to flock to the cities in subsequent decades. In addition, states and cities in the Midwest, West, and other parts of the southern United States (for example, Texas and Louisiana) were also common destinations for migrants who originated from states like Mississippi, Georgia, and the Carolinas.

From the South to the North

Common terms used for the migration into urban centers that took place at the beginning of the twentieth century include *dual migration* and the *Great Migration*. Some historians and other authors use *dual migration* to include both international and internal migration, but it has also been widely used to refer to major waves of Black migration to northern cities at different points in history. When the Great Migration is the subject, it most often refers to the migration from the South to the North, with an emphasis on the movement of Black individuals and families to escape the Jim Crow laws and discriminatory practices prevalent in the American South at the time (many of which continued well into the 1960s) and the widespread violence by whites against the Black community.

Both Black and white southerners left the South in large numbers from the beginning of the twentieth century through the 1970s. "Southern out-migration picked up right from the start of the new century, with flows accelerating in the second decade thanks to the job opportunities of World War I. By 1920, southerners living outside their home region numbered more than 2.7 million and in 1930 more than 4 million" (Gregory 2005, 13). Census data indicate that Black and white southerners made different choices as to where they settled during the sixty years between 1910 and 1970, with Black southerners more commonly settling in major urban areas, while whites from the South more commonly chose to live in suburbs or in cities other than the major ones in the Northeast and the Midwest.

One catalyst that spurred large numbers of southern Blacks to relocate to northern cities was *The Chicago Defender* newspaper and the frank assessment that its writers made regarding the prospects of life in the North versus the South. This publication, which was "a weekly Negro newspaper with its pronounced radical utterances [and] its criticism of the South . . . contributed greatly to the exodus" (Scott 1920, 29). Founded in Chicago in 1905, it was the largest-selling Black newspaper in the country. Many of the paper's readers lived in the South, where local newspapers were reluctant to criticize conditions in their own state, let alone encourage workers to depart for the North. The newspaper was in so much demand, in fact, that "its supply was usually bought up on the first day of its arrival . . . It was said that in Laurel, Mississippi, old men who did not know how to read would buy it because it was regarded as precious" (30).

Women on the Move

One significant aspect of the internal migration that took place between the Civil War and World I was the influx of wage-earning single women (both Black and white) to New York and other cities and towns. This was part of a larger trend of women entering the U.S. workforce: The women who relocated to the cities were in search of both independence and economic security, and they varied widely in their educational backgrounds and work experience. While some of these women crossed great distances to come to the cities for work, others relocated from places that were just a short train ride away.

Many female workers, single or married, found jobs in factories that produced cloth, shoes, garments, and other products, either in major city centers or mill towns. Industrialization had created a cycle of more and more people entering the workforce in order to have the cash needed to buy the increasingly abundant factory-produced goods. This trend "enticed growing numbers of women, not all of whom came from poverty, into the labor market with such effect that in 1900 five million women in the United States worked for wages and one in five U.S. workers was female" (Blackwelder 1997, 11).

Some Consequences of Internal Migration

While migration from within the United States was beneficial in many ways to both the employers and those whom they hired, this large-scale movement of people also had some negative repercussions for both the migrants themselves and the established residents. Particularly in the case of the larger waves of migration, the newcomers were often looked upon with distrust, if not hostility. In Chicago in the year 1919, for example, race riots resulted from "conflicts produced by demographic pressures [that] intensified competition for jobs and scarce housing" (Spain 2001, 43). Similar to what migrants from abroad faced, southerners who migrated northward encountered discrimination and restrictions. For Black migrants, the "color line" was all too real and translated into separation on many different levels, including which jobs, housing, and schools were open to them.

The struggles and success stories of the unprecedented movement of Blacks to the North have found ample representation in literature and the arts. Those who migrated from the South, notwithstanding the hardships they faced, made valuable contributions in many academic fields as well as in music and literature. What is known as the Harlem Renaissance, in the decades after World War I, produced authors such as Langston Hughes, Zora Neale Hurston, and James Weldon Johnson, along with musicians Duke Ellington, Cab Calloway, and Count Basie, just to name a few. Jacob Lawrence produced a series of sixty vivid paintings entitled *The Migration Series* (1940–1941). They "depicted sharecropping and lynchings in the South, families boarding northbound trains, and the injustices that migrants experienced in Northern cities" (Binder, Reimers, and Snyder 2019, 163). Panel 49 of the series shows Blacks and whites eating separately in a public place and bears this caption: "They found discrimination in the North. It was a different kind."

Women who migrated north in the late 1800s and early 1900s faced their own set of hurdles due to paternalism and discrimination based on sex, age, and marital status. "A large number of these women who lived neither in their own families nor as a domestic servant in an employer's family were labeled 'adrift' by a 1910 federal report. The majority were young and single, but some were separated, divorced, or widowed" (Spain 2001, 43). The circumstances of these women varied widely: Some were overwhelmed and either fell into poverty or returned home (if this was even feasible), while others welcomed their newfound freedom and found safe places to work and live. These symbolically "unanchored" women were widely viewed at the time as an aberration and either ostracized or viewed as in need of protection and oversight. Black women faced many of the same issues as white women, but for the former, the difficulties of adjustment were compounded by racial discrimination and a limited choice of work options compared to what their white female counterparts encountered.

WORKING AND LIVING IN THE CITIES

The rapid and unprecedented changes that major cities experienced set into motion economic and political structures that had a severe impact on the distribution of wealth in the United States. A tremendous gulf developed between what was commonly referred to either as the "upper ten percent" or "upper ten" of the U.S. population and the other social classes, even though that number was not strictly accurate. "Wealthy capitalists, manufacturers, merchants, landowners, executives, professionals, and their families made up not 'ten,' but one or two percent of the population. These were the people who owned the majority of the nation's resources and expected to make the majority of the key decisions" (McGerr 2003, 7). Those who belonged to this elite class adhered to a code that valued individuality and held that a person made his or her own fortune, literally and figuratively. "And it was just this extreme individuality that set the upper ten apart from other classes and that guaranteed social tension and conflict in the new century" (10).

In addition, the political landscape was profoundly shaped by so-called political machines, which affected nearly every aspect of urban life. Tammany Hall, a building but also the controlling organization of the Democratic Party of New York County, exerted great control over what happened in the city and how public funds were spent. A third-generation New Yorker, William "Boss" Tweed took his place within the Tammany Hall political machine. His political savvy lay in his ability to secure appointments within the Democratic Party and city government, including his position on the board of supervisors in 1858. "Tweed and his cronies became masters of 'pay to play' decades before that term was even coined. If a real estate developer wanted a street paved or improved to make his property more valuable, he had to compensate Tweed. If a business sought an edge in securing a city contract, it had to pay the 'Boss'" (Anbinder, 2016, 268). Corruption was the order of the day and alliances were formed between Tweed and other political bosses and at all levels of local and state government. In such an environment, financial and industrial interests took precedence over the needs of the residents of the cities and the nation, particularly those of the newly arrived and the poor.

Like the immigrants who came from abroad, many of the internal migrants found the conditions in which they were compelled to live and work in the cities to be, at best, unsatisfactory. This also applied to limitations imposed on them. The job market was highly stratified, depending on the applicants' social class, ethnicity, race, and whether they were internal migrants or immigrants. Once settled in cities in the North, the work that many Black men and women were able to obtain often was limited to menial service positions such as porters and maids. Office and professional jobs for Black workers tended to be either in segregated settings or nonexistent. White women had more choices in terms of the jobs open to them, but this depended on whether they were native- or foreign-born:

> Employers turned overwhelmingly to native born white women in hiring office workers or sales clerks, jobs that engaged one in ten working women in 1900. White women of native parentage predominated in the preferred jobs of accountant, bookkeeper, typist, stenographer, and office clerk, while women of foreign parentage found work as shippers, packers, and sales clerks. (Blackwelder 1997, 17)

While the major cities prided themselves on their stately mansions, row houses, and wide boulevards, neighborhoods such as the Lower East Side of New York and the South End of Boston lacked basic services, such as sanitation and access to safe food and water, particularly the poor and working class. The early wave of four million immigrants who arrived in the United States between 1820 and 1860 had caused an intense demand for housing, particularly in New York City. It was at this time that how and where people lived underwent a profound shift: "New York became a city not of 'houses' but of 'housing.' A growing proportion of its inhabitants lived in collective accommodation that was unique in the nation. This condition crossed class lines from the tenements of the poor to the increasingly dense row housing of the upper-middle class" (Plunz 2016, 4).

A tenement was technically just a multi-occupancy build-ing, but the word came to refer to the overcrowded low-rise buildings common in poor urban areas. In Manhattan, "the first tenement apartments were built in the 1860's and 1870's as a solution to the overcrowding of available housing stock . . . and until 1879, very few standards applied to tenements" (Polland and Soyer 2012, 113). Although a law attempting to impose some ground rules regarding tenements had been enacted in 1867, some historians maintain that it did little more than provide a legal definition of what a tenement was and specify some basic standards. The law proved to be ineffective, largely because its stipulations were vague and not easily enforced (Yochelson and Czitrom 2007).

Despite efforts to standardize the size and proximity of structures as well as access to air and light, the tenement build-ings were inadequate for the growing number of people they needed to accommodate. Buildings were typically four to six sto-ries high and had to fit on lots that were twenty-five by one hundred feet. Because the apartments within the tenement structures were very long and narrow, the individual dwellings were often referred to as "railroad flats." Tenement owners devised ways to further optimize the limited real estate and thus increase profits: Older structures were frequently converted to tenements by adding floors vertically and by "back building" or filling in rear-yard areas with free-standing, additional struc-tures. To worsen matters, landlords charged their tenants exor-bitant rents while failing to maintain, let alone improve, the dwellings. Children had nowhere else to play than in danger-ous and dirty streets, and lack of easy access to water meant that keeping both bodies and homes clean was a constant struggle. The 1901 Tenement Housing Act improved the situation to a certain degree, "but many of these changes came too late to affect the first generations of immigrants, who had by the turn of the century moved to other neighborhoods" (Polland and Soyer, 2012, 114–15).

On the labor front, several incidents signaled when workers in New York, Chicago, and other major cities had had enough. The Pullman Strike of 1894, the 1910 Great Revolt of cloakmakers, and the Triangle Shirtwaist Factory Fire of 1911 were just some of the cataclysmic events that drew publicity and a measure of sympathy to the plight of the worker. Throughout these years, labor unions were alternately organized, prevented, or quashed. Out of frustration, twenty-one-year old immigrant Frank Tannenbaum led three hundred homeless men on a "March of the Unemployed" on March 1, 1914, to area churches, demanding money for food and shelter. The young Tannenbaum (who was arrested not long after for a similar protest march) was gratified that he and these impoverished men were receiving attention from the press and public. He declared, "We're members of the working class . . . [and] everything in this city was created by our hands or the hands of our brothers and sisters. We have a right to share in every house and in every man's loaf of bread. What's more, we are going to make the city give it to us or take it by force" (Wallace, 2017, 747).

On March 3, 1914, three days after the March of the Unemployed, an article appeared about Tannenbaum on the front page of *The New York Times* with the headline URGES WORKERS ON TO ANARCHY (Whitfield, 2013, 97). Journalists, novelists, and political activists in the decades before and after 1914 were the ones who would shed light on and ultimately effect change on behalf of the poor and unemployed. In the end, they would speak up for those people who were too overburdened or lacked sufficient education to make their own case. Some of these individuals who exposed the conditions and inequalities of the working classes became known as "muckrakers."

PLACE NAMES AND "INVENTED BORDERS"

In the twenty-first century, many New Yorkers as well as visitors to the city are familiar with a variety of designations for the historical Lower East Side, a part of the city that has evolved into a collection of neighborhoods that have assumed different names over time. "The first name, Lower East Side, referred to New York's old working-class residential and industrial area that expanded northward in the nineteenth century as a tenement district" (Mele 2000, x). The names for the area that is east of the Bowery and Third Avenue and is bordered by Fourteenth Street on its northern side and Houston Street to the south include the East Village, Alphabet City, and Loisaida. As for the East Village: "There are no natural borders to the neighborhood, save for the East River. There are only the invented borders, whose locations and place names signify a century of cultural, political, and social struggles over neighborhood" (xii).

Loisaida is the creative name, coined in the 1970s by poet and playwright Bimbo Rivas, that was originally used to refer primarily to Avenue C, "once the vital commercial artery of the Latino/Puerto Rican neighborhood" (Abu-Lughod 1994, 26). The idea of Loisaida eventually expanded: "Once the neighborhood was claimed as 'Loisaida,' it generated a new narrative of hope for the community of Puerto Ricans in the post-industrial city" (Bagchee 2018, 106). This hope would be challenged by the waves of gentrification and displacement that followed. At times, neighborhood names have originated from those who live there and is a mark of their identity, as was the case with Loisaida, but at other times the people involved in the different struggles that are referred to above are outsiders to the area and make use of one or more labels for a particular part of the city or neighborhood for other reasons, adding to the layers of history and to the myriad stories told about these localities and their residents.

2

ANSWERING THE CALL FOR REFORM

Associations, Social Movements, and Alliances

THROUGHOUT THE NINETEENTH CENTURY in the United States, political corruption, the amassing of wealth by a small percentage of the population, and strikes and rebellions by exploited workers all contributed to an atmosphere of social unrest and frustration. What Mark Twain satirically referred to as the "Gilded Age" of the late 1880s was a time of unparalleled economic growth and the rise of the so-called robber barons. The result was a premium put on individualism over the responsibility a person owed to the larger community. Despite ample evidence that had been presented to them, the American public at the end of the nineteenth century was largely unmindful of the human costs of industrialization and unsupportive of any action the government should take: "That the municipality should assume responsibility for conditions under which its citizens lived, aside from elementary defense against disease and disorder, was considered subversive of the principles under which alone American citizenship could thrive" (Woods and Kennedy 1922, 35).

Given that U.S. society as a whole was uninformed and therefore unmoved to confront the problems facing cities and their inhabitants, it stands to reasons that others saw fit to take the reins and act. The journalists and activists called "muckrakers" opened the door by bringing attention to the political and social issues that afflicted the urban landscape and the country as a whole. In addition, similar to what had occurred in England to spark the settlement house movement, many of the calls in the United States to remedy society's ills came from churches and synagogues. Clergy in Protestant churches were among the most vocal about societal conditions and spread the Social Gospel, with its belief that "social injustice contributed to poverty, vice, and urban social dislocation" (Carson 1990, 18). The proponents of the Social Gospel maintained that the condition of the poor could not be blamed on them, but, rather, that the root causes for poverty lay with the divisions in the larger society. This view guided associations and other organizations aimed at alleviating poverty and its aftereffects, and it was also in harmony with the social reform agenda of politicians who eventually identified as Progressives. Along with neighborhood organizers and activists, many of them women, these various entities drew on an ethical foundation to work toward solving the deeply entrenched problems of the day.

It cost large sums of money to fund the buildings and operating costs of organizations like the YMCA, the Educational Alliance, and the growing number of settlement houses in New York and other cities. In addition to donations solicited by the organizations, much of the capital was provided by philanthropists of the era. The alliances that these wealthy individuals formed with those who established and were responsible for the day-to-day operations of the organizations they funded were a practical necessity. At the same time, being linked with industrialists and other power brokers raised eyebrows among the public about the motivations of the funders and what influence the donors held over those who accepted monetary help.

The goal of this chapter is to describe how journalists and others raised the call for reform and to identify the interconnections among the various groups and social movements at the close of the Gilded Age and into the Progressive Era that rose to the challenge in the belief that change was not only possible but imperative. Who were the Progressives and what did it mean to embrace a progressive social, spiritual, or political agenda at that time? In the process of answering these questions, I will describe the myriad ways in which people and organizations worked together or at least toward a common purpose in their reform efforts. The role played by women, both Black and white, in the many civic-minded groups and clubs that developed during the late nineteenth and early twentieth centuries is also highlighted. Although the settlement house movement will be touched upon here, the following chapter is devoted to the subject of settlement houses and those who worked in and depended on them.

PULLING BACK THE CURTAIN: THE CITY'S PROBLEMS ARE MADE PUBLIC

When the waves of migrants arrived in U.S cities in the nineteenth and early twentieth centuries, they encountered a perverse blend of opportunity and exploitation. As the cities filled with more and more people, increases in crime and diseases like cholera and tuberculosis increased to a point that was impossible to ignore. It is not an exaggeration to say that the cities were in need of saving (Riis 1890, Spain 2001, Steffens 1904). In addition, political corruption, the amassing of wealth by a small percentage of the population, and strikes and riots by oppressed workers had all contributed to an atmosphere of social unrest and frustration.

In light of the immense wealth and abject poverty that existed side by side in the late 1800s and the years that followed, journalists and novelists emerged and described in words, and sometimes also images, the increasingly exploitative and often illegal business practices that abounded. In addition, these writers related, in shocking detail, the plight of scores of workers and city dwellers as well as company policies that were lining the pockets of the rich. One of these journalists was Ida Tarbell, who, in a series of articles in *McClure's Magazine* from 1902 to 1904, exposed the illegal practices of Standard Oil Company and its owner, John D. Rockefeller. Tarbell's investigative reporting and published pieces ultimately led to the Supreme Court ruling that Standard Oil had violated the Sherman Anti-Trust Act. The nineteen-article series on Standard Oil took an emotional toll on Tarbell. As she explained in her autobiography:

> I asked nothing in the world but to get them into a book and escape into the safe retreat of a library where I could study people long dead, and if they did things of which I did not approve it would be all between me and the books. There would be none of these harrowing human beings confronting me, tearing me between contempt and pity, admiration and anger, baffling me with their futile and misdirected weakness. (Tarbell 1939, 239)

Another exposé came in the form of Upton Sinclair's widely read novel, *The Jungle* (1906), in which he described the miserable working conditions and unsanitary practices at meatpacking plants in Chicago. Sinclair had worked for a short time in a meat-processing plant, where he acquired direct knowledge of the gross mistreatment of animals and workers in the facility. "The Jungle appalled the public, infuriated the meatpackers, and

cut the sale of meat" (McGerr 2003, 161). Through their serial-
ized stories, essays, newspaper articles, and fictional accounts,
writers informed the public of how the rich were growing richer
while workers suffered. The overall message was that the general populace, not just those who were poor, were ultimately
being shortchanged and that this was a moral outrage.

Jacob Riis, a Danish immigrant who had experienced homelessness himself, was particularly effective in revealing the living and working conditions of the poor in New York's tenement
communities. Riis produced the photojournalistic account *How
the Other Half Lives* in 1890; it illustrated the environment in
which men, women, and children lived in their homes, places
of business, city streets, and alleyways. As a result of Riis's early
years on the streets and in his work as a police reporter, he had
developed an intimate connection with those for whom everyday life was dismal. He sketched pictures and took photographs
of such infamous sites in New York City as Mulberry Bend and
Bandits' Roost. The images are powerful and proved to be especially effective in conveying the horrendous conditions in which
many city dwellers lived. Similar to other social commentators
of the time, including the Social Gospelers, Riis did not place
the blame on the victims but, rather, on the circumstances
that had been allowed to develop and then fester. He targeted
the tenements and tenement neighborhoods in particular. He
described, street by street and room by room, not only the structures but the men, women, and children who inhabited them,
as well as the homeless.[1]

The collective efforts of Riis, Tarbell, Sinclair, and other
reformers did not go unnoticed by politicians. In 1906, Theodore Roosevelt reacted to the writers who were, in Roosevelt's
view, focusing to an unfair degree on the problems and blaming the state of affairs on corporations and politicians. He

borrowed an image from his interpretation of Bunyan's *Pilgrim Progress* of men who were so preoccupied with the "muck" that they never looked up, and thus the term *muckraking* became associated with the journalists and others who, in Roosevelt's view, were overly focused on societal problems:

> In Bunyan's Pilgrim's Progress you may recall the description of the Man with the Muck-rake, the man who could look no way but downward, with the muck-rake in his hand; who was offered a celestial crown for his muck-rake, but who would neither look up nor regard the crown he was offered, but continued to rake to himself the filth of the floor. (Roosevelt 1906)

Regardless of whether the individuals responsible for the publications that exposed living conditions and business practices liked the label of "muckraker," the words and overall message they circulated had a decided effect on the political landscape at the time and in years to come.[2] The collective effect of journalists, novelists, labor organizers, and like-minded politicians exposed the consequences of the reckless pace of urbanization and industrialization in the United States at the time. Without a sufficient number of governmental programs and initiatives to make the cities safe and habitable, others needed to fill the void and lead the charge to bring about genuine and lasting change.

FROM INDIVIDUALISM TO ASSOCIATION

Large cities in the late nineteenth and early twentieth centuries were marred by crowded neighborhoods, the exploitation of workers, many of whom were children, and lack of sanitation and clean water. Emphasis on individual achievement and excessive profit had, whether directly or indirectly, led to this state of affairs, and steps needed to be taken in order to solve the problems that industrial development had left in its wake. At the start of the twentieth century, Jane Addams, founder and head worker at the Hull House settlement in Chicago, stated, "We are passing from an age of individualism to one of association" (Addams 1902, 137).

If women wanted to exert influence in their communities beyond their immediate families before the Nineteenth Amendment to the U.S. Constitution was ratified in 1920, they needed to accomplish it by means other than casting a ballot in official elections. "Before universal suffrage, women lacked the range of civic privileges men enjoyed. Voluntary associations, however, gave them new avenues by which to pursue the public good" (Spain 2001, 3). While many women worked through places of worship to offer their services and capital to social causes, they also joined many independent associations, only some of which were based on religious principles or had ties with a religious denomination.

Since females were generally not welcome in men's clubs at the time, women formed their own groups and clubs that pursued topics and projects deemed suitable for them, including those that were concerned with what has been referred to as "municipal housekeeping." The clubs, composed at first mostly of middle-class white women, launched campaigns that included "'cleanup days,' purchasing trash buckets, giving prizes for backyard improvement, and trying to get rid of billboards. Next came beautification efforts involving tree planting, window boxes, and park benches. They soon began, however, to extend their idea of municipal housekeeping to broader aspects of civil affairs" (Stivers 2000, 50). These broader efforts eventually extended to street cleaning and garbage collection, medical care and playgrounds for children, and improved factory conditions.

One of the earliest women's clubs was the Young Women's Christian Association (YWCA), founded in 1858 in New York City. One of its initial purposes was to provide young working women with suitable housing in cities where they had no family or had not yet established a network of friends. Inspired by the Social Gospel movement, the association spread to other cities and grew to "at least 28 associations by 1875, nearly one-half of which contained boarding homes for 50 or more women" (Spain 2001, 90). The YWCA boarding facilities were eventually called "residences" to differentiate them from the many other boarding-houses available to women at the time.

Woyshner (2002) compiled a list of women's clubs established between 1869 and 1920 that illustrates the wide range of club types and their members. These organizations included the American Association of University Women, founded in 1881; the National Council of Jewish Women, founded in 1893; the National Association of Colored Women, founded in 1896; and the Women's International League for Peace and Freedom, founded in 1919. In 1890, women representing sixty-three women's clubs had attended a convention in New York City and formed, under the leadership of journalist Jane Croly, the General Federation of Women's Clubs (GFWC). Lasting contributions in the areas of education, racial equality, public health, and the rights of women were made by women's club members, many of whom went on to become social activists and public administrators.[3]

In the late 1800s and continuing for many decades, women's clubs organized by white women, almost without exception, excluded African Americans. Throughout the history of the YWCA, for example, the leadership of the organization grappled with the issue of admitting Black women into their organization and residences, but there was no systematic effort to integrate the YWCA until the 1960s. As a result, Black women needed to establish their own clubs or associations if they wished to carry out municipal housekeeping activities, receive fair wages, and work in decent conditions, or gain equal access to education. According to Lerner (1974), "Contrary to widely held racist myths, black communities have a continuous record of self-help, institution-building and strong organization to which black women have made continuous contributions" (159).

Early examples of Black women's organizations were the National Association of Colored Women (NACW), established in 1896, and the Woman's Convention (CW) Auxiliary to the National Baptist Convention, founded four years later. These two organizations established a special bond and relied in many ways on each other: "Black women's church and club work were so intertwined during the late nineteenth century that it is diffi-cult to separate their activities into religious and secular cate-gories" (Spain 2001, 83). Members of the NACW and the CW both worked to repeal the Jim Crow laws that had taken effect after the Civil War and supported antilynching legislation, reform issues that were not priorities for women's clubs whose members were predominantly white.

THE SOCIAL GOSPEL

Leaders in U.S. religious institutions, including churches, syna-gogues, and theological seminaries, also recognized the need for social reform in the late nineteenth century. Taking their cue from Samuel Barnett, an Anglican clergyman who established the first settlement house in England in 1884, Protestant clerics across the Atlantic sought ways in which they could bring together different social classes to effect much-needed change. In particular, they sought "to apply the Christian idea of service to the new challenges and the new problems of the city" (Davis 1967, 29). The message of the Social Gospel widened the scope of what was meant by salvation, called for accountability on the part of politicians and citizens, and established a new focus for the Protestant faith: Those who preached the Social Gospel conveyed to their audiences the view that the modern age had spawned serious problems and inequities in current society. As a result, church members needed to commit to "improving the lives of the working poor, lest by inaction they become complicit in perpetuating an unjust social order" (Wallace 2017, 517). This message complemented the aims of progressive reformers and the movements and institutions they fostered. Skeptics in the past and present, however, have argued that clerics as well as others who espoused the Social Gospel message were interested in converting immigrants, particularly Jews and Catholics, to the Protestant religion. I will leave this an open question for now, but the subject of religion and the settlement movement will be revisited in later chapters.

PROGRESSIVE REFORM AND PROGRESSIVISM

The social reform movement known as Progressivism took on many of the ailing cities' concerns as well as the more widespread problems that plagued the nation as a whole. The Progressive Era extended from about 1890 to the 1920s, with different phases occurring within these years and with a wide variety of actors who played their own, yet largely complementary, roles. There is debate among historians and other scholars as to the exact time span of the era as well as what the Progressives and Progressive movement actually were or wished to accomplish. Nonetheless, those politicians and private citizens who identified as progressive shared a common impulse to work against ineffective government and to channel the power of the state more effectively to serve the common good. "It began with private voluntary groups and philanthropic associations, often church-based, [which] soon realized that the problems of the new industrial order could not be solved by charity alone" (Gendzel 2011, 334). The Progressive Party was a relative latecomer to the Progressive movement. Settlement house workers, women in voluntary associations, and socially conscious writers had already been "actively involved in and working for reform in the 1890's; for them the progressive era did not begin on that day in 1901 when an assassin's bullet made Theodore Roosevelt President" (Davis 1967, xiii). Even though Roosevelt was known for his domestic progressive reforms during his tenure as a Republican president from 1901 to 1909, the Progressive Party was not formed until 1912, when Roosevelt reentered the political scene. (He had not immediately sought a third term, something that was lawfully permitted at the time.) The Progressive Party endorsed many of the same kinds of policies that Roosevelt had previously supported, and thus the party's platform was a culmination of social reform efforts that had been already been successful to a large degree and had resulted in the formation of organizations like the National Consumers League, the Child Labor Committee, and the Association of Neighborhood Workers.

The planks of the Progressive Party increased the public visibility of many of the earlier social reformers' concerns. Even though Roosevelt lost his bid for a third term as president, he and the Progressive Party supported the vote for women, the eight-hour workweek, and regulating campaign finance. Roosevelt was profoundly influenced by the work of both Jacob Riis and Jane Addams. He was moved by the words and images in Riis's book *How the Other Half Lives*, and when he was New York

City's police commissioner, Roosevelt left a note on the journalist's desk that read, "I have read your book and I have come to help" (Meacham 2018, 80). Riis's work had conveyed to Roosevelt that one could not simply read those words and remain complacent. "I believe in realizable ideals and in realizing them, in preaching what can be practiced and then in practicing it" (80). Jane Addams seconded Roosevelt's nomination at the Progressive Party's convention in Chicago in August 1912. "A great party has pledged itself to the protection of children, to the care of the aged, to the relief of overworked girls, to the safeguarding of burdened men" (93). The Progressive Party was short-lived, essentially collapsing in 1916, but the Progressive movement lived on and continued to advocate for safer working conditions, wider access to quality education and health care, and better housing.

ALLIANCES

The voluntary associations formed during the late nineteenth and the beginning of the twentieth century depended on private capital to build structures and meet their operating expenses. Although a considerable number of small donations were solicited and flowed into organizations like the settlement houses, sustaining the work on a large scale would not have been possible without large contributions from wealthy funders. Why were these philanthropists so generous and what did they expect to gain?

These are difficult questions to answer. Some of the motivation for voluntarily giving to others often comes from a sense of spiritual or ethical obligation that human beings have to be responsible stewards of what they possess. The doctrines of Christianity, Judaism, and Islam all direct the faithful to share what they have with their less fortunate brethren. Those who accepted the tenets of the Social Gospel during both the Gilded Age and the Progressive Era broadened the Christian concept of *caritas,* defined as charity or love for all, to include matters of social justice: "The Social Gospel movement applied Christian principles to the problems of daily life. It linked individual salvation to the salvation of society by focusing on such issues as workers' rights, race relations, immigration, and housing conditions" (Spain 2001, 63). Although wealthy industrialists were likely less concerned with workers' rights, at least insofar as these affected the owners' bottom line, many were cognizant of the immense good that their money could accomplish, especially if the funds were placed in the right hands for causes in which the donors believed.

Religious belief may explain the actions of some of the wealthy donors at that time. Jacob Schiff, for example, donated money to a variety of causes, including both Jewish and non-Jewish agencies and charities. A secular Jew, Schiff was the embodiment of a person who put into action *tzedakah*, a concept similar to the Christian *caritas.* In addition to the Henry Street Settlement (originally the Nurses' Settlement), he was a supporter of the Educational Alliance, a community center for immigrant youth on the Lower East Side that served a largely Jewish clientele. He also was a major donor to New York's Montefiore Hospital and Home for Chronic Invalids, as well as to such diverse educational institutions as Barnard College, the Jewish Theological Seminary, and the Tuskegee Institute (Wallace 2017).

Andrew Carnegie, the steel magnate born in Scotland, wrote an essay entitled "The Gospel of Wealth," in which he "outlined how large personal fortunes should be used to better society" (Wulfson 2001, 136). A self-avowed agnostic, Carnegie nonetheless echoed some of the themes of the Social Gospel in an essay originally published in *North American Review* in 1889, in which he declared that wealthy individuals should

> consider all surplus revenues which come to him simply as trust funds, which he is called upon to administer, and strictly bound as a matter of duty to administer in the manner which, in his judgment, is best calculated to produce the most beneficial results for the community—the man of wealth thus becoming the sole agent and trustee for his poorer brethren . . ." (Carnegie 1906, 534)

Part of what inspired Carnegie was an experience he'd had as a boy, when he was allowed to use the library of someone he knew by the name of Colonel Anderson. This act of kindness is said to have strengthened Carnegie's love for reading and sparked his desire to make books widely accessible to the public. "The impact of Colonel Anderson's generosity was not manifest until decades later, but it affected the lives of the millions of people who have used 'Carnegie libraries' since" (Payton and Moody 2008, 22). Through Carnegie's contributions to foundations that contributed to education, including teaching, the pursuit of international peace, and scientific research, he was able to impact both individual lives as well as the wider society.

Critics have pointed out that philanthropists such as Carnegie and other industrialists only made their generous charitable donations to bolster their own reputations and to deflect attention from their own often unscrupulous business and political dealings. These wealthy business owners, detractors have claimed, could highlight their good deeds and what they were providing the public in order to deflect attention from the immense profits they were accumulating and the extent to which they were trampling on workers' rights. In the view of some journalists, labor organizers, and others, Carnegie the philanthropist was only trying to redeem himself, particularly after the disastrous steelworker strike in Homestead, Pennsylvania, in 1892. Carnegie was determined to break the workers' union, but after violence ensued and ten people died, the steel tycoon initially did everything he could to distance himself from the debacle. He even tried to portray himself publicly as an owner who was in favor of fair labor practices. "Carnegie eventually expressed remorse over Homestead, but he never acknowledged his contribution to the policies that led to the tragedy" (Rees 1997, 529).

Interestingly enough, Ida Tarbell, the author who exposed the illegal business practices of John D. Rockefeller, defended the oil tycoon against claims of self-interest : "It did not take a public outcry such as came in the early years of this century against the methods of Standard Oil Company to force Mr. Rockefeller to share his wealth. He was already sharing it. Indeed, in the fifteen years before 1904 he had given to one or another cause some 35 million dollars" (Tarbell 1939, 243). Despite any ulterior motives they might have had, many of the philanthropists who financed settlement houses and other voluntary organizations and established foundations and trusts ended up making significant contributions to the public that outlived them.

CONCLUSION

The term *progressive* means different things to different people. In the late 1800s and continuing into the next century, progressive reformers brought to light conditions that were unacceptable in a democracy in which the interests of all citizens were supposed to be of value. The muckrakers exposed the squalid circumstances of many workers and their families and directed public attention to the business practices and questionable ethics of those who belonged to the "upper ten." A diverse group of people, many of them women, responded to the appeals and were determined to clean up the cities, literally and figuratively. Separate clubs for Black and white women engaged in municipal housekeeping activities and in taking care of single women who came alone to the cities. In addition, some politicians adopted many of the mandates set forth by earlier reformers, and the Progressive Party eventually emerged, even though it was short-lived. Progressive reform continued, however, and another noteworthy group of individuals put to use its energy and resources toward forming bonds with tenement dwellers and working in association with them to improve their lives—these reformers were the settlement house workers.

3

THE SETTLEMENT HOUSE

"A Place for Gathering and Distributing All the Forces of Society"

SETTLEMENT HOUSES WERE AN integral part of the Progressive movement and they created a path for future social welfare initiatives in urban areas. A number of settlement house leaders, residents, and volunteers became teachers, nurses, and social workers. Others on the local, state, and national levels fought political corruption, ended harmful child labor practices, and defended adult workers against substandard working conditions. The institutions and practices that the Progressive movement had pioneered often directly led to improvements in conditions for workers and other city dwellers, and "in these social-justice efforts, legions of activist women, despite lacking the suffrage, were enormously effective" (Nugent 2010, 1).

The concept of the settlement house traveled across the Atlantic, and the model that had been established in England was adapted to fit the circumstances of the New World, where growing immigrant communities were putting a strain on services and housing. This chapter examines the origins and significance of settlement houses during the nineteenth and twentieth centuries. The concept of the settlement house as a cooperative structure is also introduced, and I describe how these organizations were established and sustained by individuals from diverse social and religious backgrounds, with an emphasis on the crucial role that women played in the social settlement. Even though settlement houses are referred to in a generic sense, it is an essential fact that each one, along with each neighborhood in which it was situated, was unique, largely due to the responsiveness that was an essential characteristic of the individual organization.

THE SETTLEMENT HOUSE MOVEMENT

Settlement houses were instrumental in addressing the needs of the poor and collecting vital social and demographic data in U.S. cities in the late 1800s and early 1900s. Located in the middle of urban areas with the greatest need, the settlement house offered immigrant families and others free social, medical, and educational services. Residents and volunteers organized and implemented clubs as well as classes and other subjects, along with instruction in trades such as sewing and carpentry. In many of the settlement houses, residents and volunteers operated daycare facilities, kindergartens, and health clinics, taught music and music appreciation classes, and led activities in drama, poetry, and the other arts. Many of the original settlement houses throughout the country are still operating, albeit with updated programming and without resident workers.

The settlement house movement in the United States was inspired by Toynbee Hall, in London. Founded in 1884 by Samuel Barnett, an Anglican clergyman, Toynbee Hall was the first settlement house of its kind. It was located in a working-class neighborhood in East London and was a product of the newly formed Universities' Settlement Association. The residents of

Toynbee Hall, initially male university students, were charged with providing educational, recreational, and other services to poor residents in the neighborhood. A longer-range goal of the settlement house was to create a social laboratory for understanding the conditions in which the poor lived and then to "advance plans calculated to promote their welfare" (Kraus 1980, 20). After their time at Toynbee Hall, many of the young residents would go on to become landowners and legislators, and in these roles and positions of power they would be able to exert influence on social life and public opinion. Barnett was adamant that the university would have failed its students if their education did not have a positive impact on those who lived in poverty and had not been afforded the opportunity to obtain a higher education. Thus a key element in Toynbee Hall, which was emulated in many U.S. settlement houses, was to provide those in the neighborhood with "vocational and manual training, evening classes, special lecture series, [and] adult education courses in the arts and social sciences" (Reinders 1982, 45). Other settlement houses in England soon followed, including Oxford House and the Women's University Settlement; by 1911, there were forty-six settlements in Great Britain (Davis 1967).

The urban landscape of New York and other cities within the United States at the end of the nineteenth century suffered from many of the same ill effects of industrialization as London. Two of the most pressing of these were crushing poverty and widespread abuse of workers, including children. Many of the individuals and groups who eventually established and staffed settlement houses in New York and other U.S. cities had traveled to London to observe the social experiment that was Toynbee Hall and to learn about the settlement movement there. Among the many American visitors to Toynbee Hall were Stanton Coit, who founded the Neighborhood Guild (later called the University Settlement) with Charles Stover and Carl Schurz in New York City in 1886, and Christina MacColl of Christodora House, who also made a trip there. Jane Addams, founder of Hull House in Chicago in 1889, had visited Toynbee Hall on three separate occasions. "The Atlantic served not only as a highway for trade, travelers, and immigrants, but also as a bridge for ideas and institutions" (Reinders 1982, 39).

Despite the differences in their histories and class system structures at the time, settlement house founders and workers in both North America and Britain sought to create communities that more closely approached the ideals of social justice and human equality. The settlement house brought together the privileged and the poor in order to confront the disparities experienced by the latter, both in quality of life and security of livelihood. In the United States, "most settlement workers were under the age of thirty, and about 90 percent were university or college educated. Some of the men involved in the movement had studied theology and had originally intended to enter ordained Christian ministry" (Stebner 2006, 1062). As had been the case in Europe, young people in North America were tapped to confront social problems directly by living among those most affected by the conditions in the crowded urban centers of that time.

Building on the Toynbee Hall model, the settlement movement in the United States quickly took root throughout the nation, growing from seventy-four in the year 1897 to over four hundred in 1910 (Batlan 2005). Settlement houses in New York and other U.S. cities were primarily located in areas settled by immigrants. In the late 1800s and early 1900s, the newcomers who lived on the Lower East Side hailed largely from Eastern and Southern Europe. This was a departure from the population in the original settlement house in the East End of London.

Many of the neighbors of Toynbee Hall had lived for generations in poverty, while the majority of city dwellers who utilized the services of U.S. settlement houses were adapting to an entirely alien way of life, and for many, the poverty in which they found themselves was a new experience. These immigrants needed to be able to speak English, learn to function in a new cultural and social environment, and secure gainful employment. This was difficult to do alone.

Those who established U.S. settlement houses, as well as their successors, aspired not only to create a community of inhabitants from different social classes and circumstances but also to ensure that the relationship was a reciprocal one. In the U.S. settlement house, it was crucial that the work stem directly from the needs of the community. From its inception, those involved with the settlement movement insisted that their work was not paternalistic charity or handouts and that settlement house workers were different from the "upper class ladies in the United Kingdom and United States who practiced 'friendly visiting' with poor families in the nineteenth century, expecting that their manners and advice would help cure the illness of poverty" (Payton and Moody 2008, 44).

The ideal relationship between settlers and their neighbors was one of mutual respect and open communication. Workers in settlement houses were not providing services unilaterally and then walking away; rather, they were expected to genuinely learn from the experience and then act on it. The settlement houses in the United States, compared to those in England, were more likely to serve women and children, but this did not preclude them from also offering programs and services to adult males. The enthusiasm of the settlement house residents and what they had to offer their neighbors were welcomed eagerly by these neighbors, especially the youngest among them: "The children and adolescents swarmed in and stretched the settlers' resources and imagination to their limits." Much to the residents' delight, they discovered "that [the settlement houses'] clubs, classes, kindergartens, and summer camps formed a backbone of continuity that ensured settlement survival not just year to year, but over decades" (Carson 1990, 52).

An important aspect of both the genesis and day-to-day operations of the settlement house movement is the role that religion, especially Christianity, played in settlement houses in Britain and the United States. The Anglican clergyman and the founder of Toynbee Hall, Samuel Barnett, espoused a social consciousness shared by other clergy at that time who "moved beyond traditional church philanthropy to formulate a theological imperative for social action" (Carson 1990, 3). The doctrine of the Social Gospel that took hold in the United States had a decided effect on the organization and work of settlement houses. In principle, the Social Gospel was based on broad tenets that did not proselytize for any one faith, but in practice it was deeply influenced by Christianity.

The extent to which religion and religious ideology permeated the settlement house movement was a point of contention in the past and remains so to this day. The staff at Christodora, as well as at the other settlement houses, held, by and large, "many shades of opinion concerning religion in the settlement" (Carson 1990, 57). Settlement workers, in contrast to those who worked at religious missions or church-sponsored settlements, generally resisted the notion that they were proselytizing, although "the values embedded in the Protestant culture most of them sprang from inevitably shaped the settlement idea" (57). In some settlement houses, practices such as singing religious hymns or putting up a Christmas tree raised red flags for some members of the local communities, and it was reported that

Jacob Riis and Jacob Schiff came into conflict about such issues and that Lillian Wald was called in to act as intermediary between the two men at one point (219).

Some settlement house head workers, such as Lillian Wald and Jane Addams, made it a point to try to avoid bringing religious symbolism and practices that might be alien or offensive to others into the settlement house. Others, like Christina Mac-Coll, for example, for whom faith was intrinsic to her identity, saw religion as an intensely personal matter that could not help but permeate all aspects of her life: "We live out the life of the Lord Jesus Christ, or let Him live it through us, without any anxious questioning of whether others will ever see from our standpoint or not" (MacColl 1903).

A COOPERATIVE STRUCTURE

A cooperative is a particular type of organization that exists throughout the world. There are cooperatives created by farmers, artists, and other groups of individuals who share a particular profession, talent, or activity. In a technical sense, a cooperative is a legal entity in which members share ownership and cooperatively distribute any earnings that may result from their enterprise. Although the goal is to benefit members and be economically viable, the modern-day cooperative also has distinct social and philosophical goals:

> Although cooperative efforts of various sorts have existed since the beginning of civilization, the modern movement began primarily as a response to industrial capitalism. Then, those concerned about the problems created by industry looked to a variety of private and public efforts to provide greater security and equity to those whose lives were being shaped and reshaped by powerful economic changes. (Battilani and Schröter 2012, 2)

Some groups refer to themselves as a cooperative simply on the basis of the egalitarian principles that underlie their work, but without there being any legal agreement or formal organization. They may identify themselves as a cooperative because they share a set of values and practices that guide what they do and how they relate to one another. This type of cooperative organization may lack the attributes of joint ownership and cooperative distribution of earnings or even equal voting rights, but they may still emphasize the fundamental values of fairness and equality. Individuals involved in settlement house work were unquestionably committed to the ideas of fairness and equality, and they were determined to establish enterprises that were sustainable, albeit with the objective of fostering a relatively abstract type of prosperity.

I propose that the settlement house be viewed as a "cooperative structure" that consists of the settlement house workers, volunteers, and their neighbors, as well as the patrons who supported the settlements financially and otherwise. This kind of structure was not a physical building but, rather, consisted of an assemblage of people involved in an organization and associated activities that were beneficial to all. In his book on the settlement house movement in New York City, Kraus (1980) characterized those who took up the cause of the settlement house as "practical idealists" and maintained that "the '3Rs' of the settlement movement were residency, research, and reform" (131).

An important point about cooperation in the context of the settlement house movement is that working together toward common objectives was both a social and a political act. "The settlement sought to forge sympathetic, militant cooperation within the urban social organism" (Bender 2008, 9). In this sense, cooperation can be seen as a focused effort, relying on like-minded members, fierce in its intensity, and with specific objectives in mind. In *Twenty Years at Hull-House*, published in 1910, Jane Addams devoted an entire chapter to the subject of "civic cooperation." She described the everyday struggles and what she called "wretchedness" that residents witnessed in the settlement house neighborhoods. Settlement house workers, along with and on behalf of their neighbors, combatted these conditions through such actions as filing petitions, conducting community-based campaigns, and becoming municipal board members. In Chicago, they also allied themselves with organizations such as the Juvenile Protective Association, advocating for youth when this vulnerable population had no other voice.

Residents who lived in the settlement house might have also engaged in outside work, and shorter-term residents were supervised by those who had worked there for a longer period of time (Kraus 1980). At least one person was appointed as the head worker, many of whom had also been responsible for establishing that settlement house or had been somehow involved in it from its inception. In many settlement houses, the head worker, especially when that person had occupied the position for many years, was synonymous with the organization. Two of these, Jane Addams of Hull House in Chicago and Lillian Wald of the Henry Street Settlement in New York City, were active in their respective settlements for much of their lives and enjoyed recognition for their work, nationally and internationally, and for their support of a range of social causes.

Some settlement workers and outside observers have suggested that the settlement house operated under a relatively loose hierarchy, while others have a different view of the chain of command in the settlement house: "The head resident exerted great influence in establishing the tone of the house and often was responsible for recruiting its residents. Settlement houses were hierarchical in structure, although some operated with a degree of mutual decision making among co-residents" (Stebner 2006, 1061). As was true of other aspects of settlement house life, the relationships between the head worker and the other settlers varied, depending on the number of workers, the head worker's personality and years of experience, and the prevailing philosophy of that particular settlement house.

"WOMEN MARRIED THE SETTLEMENT. MEN DID NOT."

Although a large number of U.S. settlement houses were staffed by both men and women, the contribution made by females in the establishment and operation of Christodora and many other settlement houses was significant and, in many cases, longer lasting than that of their male counterparts. As I delved into the history of the settlement house movement in the United States, it became apparent to me that the part women played in the movement was a complex topic and controversial subject. Carson (1990), for example, voiced the view that "the American settlement movement was not exclusively a women's movement" and that "it is impossible to quantify meaningful differences between the personal motives actuating the men and women entering the settlement houses" (49). In terms of comparable numbers, Carson held that women at different points in settlement history numerically outnumbered men, an assessment echoed by Stivers (1991), who stated that "between 1886 and 1914, 60 percent of settlement residents were women" (59).

Access to postsecondary education had left many middle- and upper-class white women upon graduation unwilling to return to the kind of sheltered private life that was common for women of their social class at that time. A group of female graduates from Smith College founded the College Settlements Association (CSA) in New York City in 1890, which was just one year after the College Settlement on Rivington Street, on the Lower East Side, had been established by Vida Scudder and Jean Fine. A devout Christian and staunch socialist, Scudder was involved in the settlement house movement for most of her adult life in both New York and Boston.[1]

The CSA had chapters at colleges that included Radcliffe, Barnard, Smith (Vida Scudder's alma mater), and Wellesley, all of which were well-known, elite women's institutions. The CSA wanted "to establish, support, and exercise general control over settlements, train women for social service, and accomplish educational work of a broad scope" (Spain 2001, 114). Engaging in the work of the settlement formed a bridge between the education that these women had received and serving a useful purpose outside of the home, where traditionally they would have been expected to return after college. In addition, the development of social science as a legitimate discipline in the United States made it possible for social conditions and problems to be brought into focus, studied, and analyzed. "The settlement house movement provided an opportunity for women to directly witness the conditions under which poor immigrants lived, learn of the struggles and difficulties, and to see firsthand the effects of unjust policies and laws. The reaction to these injustices grew into an activism that would have repercussions for generations to come" (Sofge 2004, 23).

Colleges, especially those that belonged to the CSA, encouraged their female students to take up residence in urban settlement houses, and the settlement houses were happy to receive them. As alien as the urban neighborhoods could be to these young women, the settlement house was an enclave where they felt safe and were surrounded by like-minded individuals. There was a kind of familiarity for many of them who had come from these small private colleges, where women often lived in "cottages" as relatively self-contained units. At some schools, peers recruited their friends to go live in the urban settlement houses, and the result was that large numbers of current students or graduates volunteered at the same time or in consecutive years.

In a survey of forty-four individuals who were settlement house workers in New York City between the years of 1886 and 1914, Kraus (1980) made some comparisons between female head workers and their male counterparts. He reported that the thirteen women head workers in the survey averaged twenty-four years of service in the movement, while male head workers averaged only eight years performing that work. Stivers (2000) similarly reported that men were more likely to take on settlement house work when they were in their twenties and then embark on marriage and a career outside the settlement. It should be noted, however, that many of these males were subsequently involved in social reform efforts and/or government service and in these roles carried on the social mission of the settlement house.

When all of the workers in Kraus's survey were taken into account, "of the 21 women considered, only two were married," which led the author to make the statement "Women married the settlement. Men did not" (142). Information gathered on the thirteen female settlement house head workers in the survey revealed that their average age at the time of the survey was twenty-nine and only two of them were married. We know from other records and news stories that at least three of the head workers who were specifically mentioned on that list—namely, Christina MacColl, Lillian Wald, and Emilie Wagner (of the Third Street Music School Settlement on the Lower East Side) never married. Another source reports that even though the average time that a female resident remained at the settlement house was about three years, unmarried women remained for an average of ten years (Stivers 2000).

The prevalence of unmarried women who lived in settlement houses for long periods of time has led to speculation about the sexual orientation of these women. "Single settlement women often established their most significant emotional and personal relationships with other women. Boston marriages— referring to two women living together in long-time unions—were rather common among career settlement women. Such relationships were probably both platonic and romantic . . ." (Stebner 2006, 1062). It is important to consider the time period in which these women lived in the late nineteenth century and early twentieth and to refrain from placing them in categories that are more in line with current views regarding sexuality and sexual identity.

Lillian Faderman, author of the book *Surpassing the Love of Men,* noted that her friends in the 1970s and early 1980s were struggling with the concept of "romantic friendship"; in other words, that there can be nonsexual relationships between two adults, especially two who share the same living space for protracted periods of time. "Their difficulty, it appeared to me, had to do with their assumption that what is true of behavior and attitudes today has been true at all times" (Faderman 1981, 18). Nearly two decades later, Faderman looked back and clarified what she hoped she had accomplished with that earlier work: "The book attempts to make clear through historical documentation the extent to which sexuality and affectionality had been fluid and flexible in other eras. It challenges notions of the stability of sexual identity and it supplies evidence that identity based on sexuality became a phenomenon relatively recently in modem history" (Faderman 1999, 26).

At the time that settlement houses were founded and then flourished in the United States, an attitude termed by historians as "the cult of true womanhood" was pervasive in both the United States and Great Britain. According to this viewpoint, a woman's place was in the home, and she was not suited to public life or the competitive nature of the business world. This mind-set, ironically enough, served only to fuel some of the women who ultimately joined the settlement house movement, particularly those who were college-educated. Muncy (2006) described these women as "bruised by constraints on their aspirations and ready to unfetter their capacities for personal independence and public authority" (3). At the same time, the energies of some settlement women were guided by roles accorded to them by society as guardians of public virtue and as civic or municipal housekeepers. It only seems logical then that acting in those capacities supplied women with "the moral authority both to act directly and to advocate government action" (Stivers 2000, 61) and also gave many of them the confidence they needed to enter into public service.

NONRESIDENT VOLUNTEERS AND THE SETTLEMENT HOUSE

Not all of the men and women who devoted their energy and talents toward settlement house work were settlers who lived in the buildings. Many were also volunteers who lived outside the settlement itself and worked in various capacities for either the short or long term. These individuals, similar to the house residents, often came directly from colleges and universities, while others were recruited by workers or individuals familiar with the settlement house.

Ellen Gould, the recipient of Helen Schechter's letters and a teacher of English, is listed in the annual reports of Christodora House as a volunteer for several years. Even after returning home to Minnesota, Gould made financial donations to the settlement house. Teaching English was an important function of many of the settlement houses, both in terms of providing an opportunity for immigrants to develop language proficiency as well as serving as a means of assimilation into American life. Classes in English and vocational skills such as sewing, typing, and carpentry helped open doors for many immigrant newcomers, although they often still had to contend with anti-immigrant sentiment outside the settlement house, no matter how well they spoke the language or how qualified they were for work.

Another nonresident volunteer at a settlement house was Eleanor Roosevelt. A lifelong activist for a range of social causes, she was made aware of social inequities when she volunteered at the College Settlement at the age of nineteen. She had been brought there by another student from Barnard College, and Eleanor offered her talents at teaching calisthenics and dance to neighborhood children (Wallace 2017). On the occasion of the College Settlement's sixtieth anniversary, Roosevelt remarked that the experience "had been a lesson in human cooperation and enterprise" (Kraus 1980, 131). Volunteerism remains essential to those settlement houses still in existence as well as to the community organizations that have arisen from them over the years.

BEHIND THE SCENES

A description of those who were responsible for the founding and operation of the settlement houses in the United States would not be complete without mentioning some of the people who provided them with financial support. Examining the Christodora House records, it became clear that there were myriad contributors to that enterprise and that they came from all walks of life. Most of these donors gave money, while others provided supplies, food, and other material necessary to the settlement house and summer camp operations. Soliciting funds was a constant chore for head workers and settlement house board members, especially during and subsequent to economic downturns like the Wall Street Crash in 1929 and the ensuing Great Depression.

In addition to the smaller donors, there were also philanthropists who single-handedly provided significant financial support to individual settlement houses. Jacob Schiff financially supported Lillian Wald's activities first by providing generous support to the developing Visiting Nurse Service, supposedly at the urging of his mother-in-law. Schiff purchased the building at 265 Henry Street, which became the site of the Henry Street Settlement, and he remained one of its major benefactors (Wallace 2017). Two other philanthropists who contributed significantly to individual settlement houses were Arthur Curtiss James and his wife, Harriet. The subject of both a book and a movie (Vaughan 2019, 2017), James inherited his father's mining business and eventually evolved into a railway tycoon, "controlling ownership of about 40,000 miles of railroad track—about one-seventh of the entire network in the country—when he died" (Flynn 2019). Like Jacob Schiff, Arthur Curtiss James donated widely to causes in which he and his wife deeply believed, one of which was Christodora House. The James family provided the financing for the "skyscraper settlement" building that Christodora House was to inhabit on Avenue B, dedicated in 1928, and Harriet was on the settlement house board for many years. Arthur Curtiss James left a large sum of money when he died, in 1941, to the James Foundation, which contributed to a wide range of charities, and similarly, when she died, Harriet James left $100,000 each to Christodora House and the YWCA, as well as $50,000 to Smith College.[2]

A PLACE FOR ALL

Finally, the settlement house existed because of the people in its neighborhood. Who were these individuals and families who joined the clubs, enrolled in the classes, and attended the classes and public readings? The settlement house as a social service agency and gathering place was largely a haven for poor families, many of whom had recently immigrated to the United States. Those who settled on the Lower East Side in New York City were Italian, Irish, Greek, Hungarian, Polish, Romanian, Russian, Slovak, and Ukrainian, among other nationalities. This demographic profile was mirrored in many other U.S. cities. Families in particular were the ones who benefited from the settlement houses' playgrounds, medical clinics, clubs for both adults and children, and summer camps in the countryside. A summary of activities undertaken by Kingsley House in New Orleans, founded to serve a neighborhood of Irish, German, and Italian immigrants in 1896, underscores the importance of the settlement house to the quality of life in the neighborhood:

> [The settlement] conducted an investigation into housing conditions; opened the first public playground in New Orleans; turned a vacant lot used as a dump into a garden; [and] carried on an investigation into the causes of tuberculosis. The doctors connected with its clinic made a house to house canvass [sic] of the neighborhood and collected data concerning hygiene, sanitation, and family health. (Woods and Kennedy 1911, 91).

Kinglsey House was also noteworthy for starting the first programs for the sight-impaired in Louisiana in the early 1900s and later racially integrating its programs in the 1950s, "when it was illegal to do so" (Price 2011).

During the course of my research, I also came upon a work written by Bernard Warach that comprises over six hundred pages: *Hope: A Memoir* (2011). Warach was part of a boys club that met at Christodora House when he was in high school, and he went on to become a social worker and ultimately establish the Jewish Association for the Aged in New York. Details of his life as well as that of Helen Schechter, another club member at Christodora House, will be presented in the chapter on the early years of that settlement house.[3]

CONCLUSION

Both men and women found, in social settlement work, a way to connect with other humans across class lines. These experiences and relationships led many settlement house workers to take on the herculean task of seeking and implementing remedies for the social issues of the day on the local, state, and national levels. Those who committed to the important work of the settlement house, many of whom were women, made use of their own talents, education, and time to bring attention to the needs of society's most vulnerable members.

A strong case can be made that settlement houses and community centers were, and still are, very much needed. A statement by the University Settlement on Eldridge Street, the first in the country and still operating after 135 years, sums it up well: "Settlement Houses have never been more relevant. The model, because it evolves, remains evergreen. Our history informs us but does not bind us. We honor it. As our neighborhoods change, we change. And as our neighbors shape our work, and our efforts help shape public policy, our city changes—for the better" (University Settlement Society). At the end of the day, the greatest significance of the settlement house has been its positive impact on the scores of people of all ages who were welcomed into the house and availed themselves of the facilities and wide range of activities. Settlements and community houses in New York and other cities continue to provide programs and services that help combat poverty and work to promote social justice locally and nationally. In the settlement house clubs, classes, and other activities, participants gained knowledge and skills that they could carry with them into and beyond the neighborhood. "People came to the settlement house because they needed what it had to offer. For people who had no alternative, the weekly health clinic was an important resource. For children of the city, the settlement playground, with its grass and seesaws, was better than the streets" (Crocker 1992, 224).

PART II

CHRISTODORA OVER THE DECADES

4

FROM THE YOUNG WOMEN'S SETTLEMENT TO CHRISTODORA HOUSE, 1897–1948

I saw a beautiful thing last night—
Tired women dancing underneath a light,
Hand on hip, indomitable, gay,
After the day's work they danced the night away.
—Margaret Widdemer, n.d., excerpt from "Dancers"

SOME SETTLEMENT HOUSES IN the United States were able to achieve iconic status because of the groundbreaking work they did and how they improved life in the cities and advocated for families in their neighborhoods. Lillian Wald, Jane Addams, Graham Taylor, and a handful of other settlement house leaders also became known nationally and internationally for their impact on social policy, especially in the areas of health, labor, and social policy. Many people in the United States today are familiar with the Henry Street Settlement in New York or Hull House and Chicago Commons in the Midwest. However, many other settlement houses that served their neighborhoods in cities across this country are not as well known, and the organizations themselves, may, if they have not survived in one form or another, have faded from memory.

Christodora House was one of the lesser-known but nonetheless vital settlement houses in the United States. The organization and its founders did not achieve widespread fame and they receive only a brief mention, if any, in the books and articles on the settlement house movement in the nineteenth century and early twentieth century. When the name Christodora is brought up today, it is likely to have other meanings and associations. Christodora may be familiar to some people as the organization that conducts environmental and educational programs for youth in New York City. Others may know about the Christodora House building at 143 Avenue B and its individually owned condominium apartments. That same Christodora House, the sixteen-story structure that towers over Tompkins Square Park in what is now called the East Village, also played a central role in protests over gentrification in the 1980s. Finally, Christodora House may be known to history and architecture enthusiasts for its place on the State Register and the National Register of Historic Places since 1986.

What may not be known is that the Christodora settlement house had a tremendous impact on the surrounding community and nearby neighborhoods on the Lower East Side. Beginning in 1897, Christina MacColl and Sara Carson and scores of settlers and others who volunteered their time were responsible for providing men, women, and children in the neighborhood with a wide variety of educational, health, and occupational services they otherwise would have done without. In addition, Christodora House, through its clubs, performances, and publications, made a lasting impression on cultural life and the arts in New York. The excerpt from Margaret Widdemer's poem at the beginning of this chapter is just one example of a work that was available to the public through the Poets' Guild at Christodora House, an organization that sought to instill a love of poetry in young and old.

Chronicled here is a history of the many facets of Christodora House, with a focus on the years from 1897 to 1948. Two key components of its history are the workers, many of whom were women, and the programs and activities they made available to their neighbors. Health and dental clinics, day trips within and outside New York City, and public space for drama and musical performances were just some of what Christodora House made available to the adults and children in the area. Another important part of Christodora's story is that the "skyscraper settlement" at 143 Avenue B was only one of several physical locations where Christodora House operated, and that other ones included the basement of a delicatessen, the Jacob Riis Houses, and several other buildings on the Lower East Side and in neighboring areas.

Settlement houses also provided their neighbors with opportunities for recreation, physical activity, and connecting with nature. There was an acute need for recreational facilities in crowded urban neighborhoods, and the gymnasium and swimming pool in Christodora's sixteen-story building (constructed in 1928) were precious resources they shared with settlement house club members and other children and groups from within and beyond the Tompkins Square Park area. Outside the city, Christodora House owned a sprawling camp in the Watchung Hills of New Jersey, where the settlement house linked the children and families of the Lower East Side of New York City with nature and the kinds of experiences that more affluent New Yorkers took for granted. The important role that Northover Camp played in Christodora's philosophy and activities would prove to be vital to the resilience and longevity of the organization.

Figure 4.1. Christodora House on Tompkins Square in New York City, ca. 1929. Christodora House Collection, Rare Book and Manuscript Library, Columbia University.

The 1930s and 1940s were the last years in which workers at Christodora House lived on-site, a hallmark of the original settlement houses. The Depression, which lasted from the late 1920s until just before the onset of World War II, took a toll on the resources that any one social service organization could offer. This was also the case in the years during both world wars. Even though the federal government was able to sponsor some programs like the Federal Music Project at Christodora and other settlement houses, these initiatives ended just as suddenly as they had begun when government resources shifted. Staff members at Christodora were busily coping with current conditions while keeping an eye on what might lie around the corner. During the 1930s and 1940s, the settlement house was still providing vital services as well as educational and moral support to its neighbors at the building on Avenue B, but sweeping changes were soon to come.

Finally, I delve into the overarching theme of "practical idealism" as it applies to settlement houses in general and Christodora in particular. Christina MacColl and the other workers at the settlement house recognized the urgent need for medical and dental facilities in the neighborhood, so they established their own clinics and collaborated with the Red Cross to make Christodora the site of an official health station. The combination of practicality and idealism also motivated the decision to include a multistory residence in the 143 Avenue B building, a space that had the potential to generate enough income to enable the settlement to become self-sustaining.

The source of much of the information here has come from the archives of Columbia University, a collection that is a rich source of information and details on the origins as well as the day-to-day business of running a settlement house. The materials also offer valuable insight into the people who made

Christodora House possible over the many decades of its existence. The letters, scrapbooks, club minutes, and annual reports in the boxes of records document the triumphs and challenges that the settlement house workers experienced and how, against tremendous odds, they transformed the lives of thousands of New Yorkers. What is all the more remarkable is that Christodora, as well as the other settlement houses in New York City and across the country, accomplished this despite a perennial lack of funding, the influenza epidemic of 1918, economic depressions, two world wars, and the rise and fall of a great many political careers. What follows is a description of how they were able to do this.

THE BEGINNINGS

Christina Isobel MacColl, the daughter of a Presbyterian minister, was born in 1864 and raised in upstate New York. She attended the Emerson College of Oratory in Boston, whose mission was to "build up and strengthen the entire individuality, to open the mouth of the spirit and put self in the right relation with the universe" (Hopkins 2011).[1] As a result of her religious beliefs and education, MacColl was a staunch advocate of social service and lifelong learning.

After Christina MacColl moved to New York City in 1893, she worked for the Harlem branch of the YWCA, where she met Sara Carson. The two of them were intrigued by the concept of the settlement house and excited at the prospect of living in the city and working closely with their neighbors. Carson had grown up in New York and New Jersey in a Quaker family, but when she reached adulthood, she embraced "the more hierarchical structure of the Presbyterian church" (Yee 2011, 143). MacColl and Carson were ideal recruits for the Social Gospel message, having been strengthened in their resolve to learn and work alongside the poor by a visit to England's Toynbee Hall. This was the same journey many settlement house leaders in the United States made, one that reinforced their determination to establish a settlement house once they returned home.

In a memorial to Christina MacColl after her death, the writer explained that settlement house work was relatively new in the years prior to 1897, "and the Association [the YWCA] did not see its way to support it" (Christodora House Collection 1939). Consequently, MacColl and Carson left their jobs to pursue this new project. "The idea was to give the girls of an immigrant group, diverse in race and creed, a social center that should be tolerant, educationally effective, and conducted without evasion on a truly religious, non-sectarian basis" (Christodora House Collection 1939). In a book about Chicago's Hull House, the author observes that an underlying value of settlement houses was religion but that "religion was not defined according to creed or institution, but in terms of exploring the totality of life" (Stebner 1997, 34).

MacColl and Carson identified the area downtown near Tompkins Square Park as a perfect location for a place that would serve young immigrant women in the neighborhood. The two of them aspired to provide classes and activities identified by the neighborhood women themselves instead of outsiders dictating choices to them. In recalling the reasons for locating what was to become the Christodora settlement house in this part of the Lower East Side, Christina MacColl related that a local Protestant minister had appealed to her and Sara Carson to establish an organization for people in the area, since his church had not been successful in attracting them:

> We chose this neighborhood because it was the most thickly
> populated part of the city (of which we knew) without a settle-
> ment. Also because a clergyman of this neighborhood said, "We
> are not meeting the various religions in this part of the city. All
> about us are Jews and Catholics of all nationalities who will not
> come near our churches and missions. We are touching but a
> handful of even the German Protestants. I hope you will locate
> here and see if you can reach the people." This afforded just the
> encouragement we needed. (MacColl 1903)

The choice of the Tompkins Square area for a settlement house
made sense logistically as well. "When it opened in 1897, Christodora House was the only settlement in New York's Sixth
Assembly District, an area of the Lower East Side rife with social
and economic problems. Fifty-five percent of the inhabitants
(54,714) were foreign-born, and the neighborhood supported the
greatest concentration (4,000 per block) of immigrants in the
United States" (Hopkins 1999, 37).

In June 1897, Christina MacColl and Sara Carson carried
through with their plan. In an account of the history of Christodora House told to an audience of house residents decades later,
MacColl recalled how she and Sara Carson had rented a back portion of a delicatessen at 163 Avenue B for a reading room. They
had also leased three rooms above it as living quarters for themselves. The meetings would be held in the cellar of the establishment, some of which was partitioned off and used as a storeroom
for limburger cheese and sauerkraut. Another part of the cellar
was used for storing coal. MacColl reminisced, "In those days
when the coal was put in, the dust was terrific. In fact we were
pioneers in using coal dampening. But, our friends, we—believe it
or not—had a glorious time" (Christodora House Collection 1933).

Despite enthusiasm and high hopes, MacColl and Carson were unsure whether anyone would show up at the initial meeting, scheduled for a Thursday night. It would turn out that they had correctly gauged the need for what would eventually become a settlement house in the area, despite the sketchiness of their preliminary plans. The attendance that first night, combined with how successful they were in attracting people to the settlement over the years, confirmed that there was indeed a great interest in what the two young women had to offer.

> We had 98 our first night. We did not know whether we would have anybody. We did not know how to get people to come . . . Miss Carson finally hit on the idea of taking a sheet of heavy brown paper and on that she wrote (I shall never forget the words; I hope I can get it just right), "Will all girls over 16 who live in this neighborhood welcome us this evening at 8. You are all invited. Free." (Christodora House Collection 1933)

At that first meeting, when asked what they would like to do at that location every week, one woman said that she would "like to know how to make a decent hat." MacColl recalled that fifty young women signed up that night for a millinery class, while another in the audience expressed interest in a class in dressmaking, and one was established. In addition, MacColl related that one of the girls in attendance had said, "'My mother would like to have me learn that thing you play on all day like a piano only it doesn't make any noises; it writes letters.' She meant a typewriter, so we formed a class in that" (Christodora House Collection 1933). From the vantage point of forty-two years later, MacColl pointed out that one of the young women who had been in that first typing class went on to work as secretary to the mayor of New York for three administrations.

THE PEOPLE

Every settlement house required many individuals to keep it running every day and enough financial capital to pay the bills. Christodora House was made possible by Christina MacColl and Sara Carson and a rotating staff of other resident workers, along with the support of members who paid nominal fees (if any), donors, volunteers, board members, and, after 1928, those who were referred to as "club residents." From 1928 to 1948, the sixteen-story building contained a residence on the upper floors for local young students and professionals who were not settlers in the usual sense. This was a unique feature intended to help the settlement house generate income, although the residents were also encouraged to volunteer their time to settlement work when they could. Some reports indicate that the residents on the upper floors even received a reduction in rent in return for their service.

Additional staff in the Christodora House building was needed to keep the premises in order and prepare food, along with clinic workers, nurses, and lawyers who worked for the settlement house, either full-time or part-time. Also associated with Christodora House were some remarkable artists and bene-factors through the years, people who selflessly lent their time and talents to Christodora's activities, classes, and public programming in literature, art, music, and drama, in some instances breaking ground and putting New York on the cultural map.

Christina MacColl and Sara Carson

Christina MacColl, like some of the other settlement founders, identified herself her whole life as the "head worker" of Christodora House, rather than as the director or manager, and was officially listed on annual reports and other documents as "Head Resident Worker." She fulfilled that role until a few years before her death, in 1939, and was the face of Christodora House for many years. At MacColl's Memorial Service, Edward Steiner recalled the effect of her presence: "Her face was unforgettably impressive, like that of a monarch on a coin. There was something regal in her face, commanding in her figure, her posture erect, her features so strong, her eyes so penetrating and yet so kindly, so penetrating and truth compelling, that you never could put anything over on her. You couldn't very well tell a lie in her presence" (Steiner 1939).

Less visible in the operations of Christodora House after the initial years was Sara Carson. Although Carson was one of the cofounders, she left New York not long after it was established. She relocated to Toronto, Canada, where she helped establish Evangelia House in 1902 in a storefront building in a working-class neighborhood, the first settlement house in that city (James 2001). This was just five years after Christodora House was founded. Ten years later, Carson launched St. Christopher House, also in Toronto, a settlement house that was associated with the Presbyterian Church. There is no record of a disagreement between the two cofounders, but based on Sara Carson's short initial tenure at Christodora House and the nature of her work in Canada, it appears that Carson might have preferred to be associated with a settlement house that was officially a "Christian settlement," which was the case for both Evangelia House and St. Christopher House.

The "Settlers"

In order to fulfill the aim of the settlement house and to be considered a true settler, workers were required to live in the house and contribute actively to its operation, whether this meant assisting in the clinic, teaching classes, supervising recreational activities, or any number of other responsibilities. "Involvement in the movement gave participants a sense of importance and a sense of contributing to a cause greater than themselves" (Stebner 2006, 1062). Christina MacColl and Sara Carson were the two original settlers at Christodora House, living upstairs in the building where they held their first meetings for the young women in the neighborhood.

Christodora's annual reports recorded different numbers of resident settlement house workers and volunteers, depending on the year. "By 1902, 13 women residents lived at Christodora House and, when a building for boys was purchased in 1905, they were joined by three male residents" (Blunt 2008, 556). The 1911 *Handbook of Settlements* reported that there were thirteen settlers who lived in the Christodora House building (nine women and four men) and four volunteers (one woman and three men) that year. In 1923, a similar number, nine women and three men, were in residence. That same year, thirty-nine non-resident volunteers (twenty-four men and fifteen women) were working at Christodora. This last tally is the only record I have seen where male workers at Christodora House outnumbered female ones, although the majority of men in this case were volunteers and not resident settlers. The numbers of both residents and volunteers increased after the building constructed in 1928 provided more room and facilities for activities and greater living space for resident workers and others.

The women and men who worked at Christodora and other New York settlement houses were typical of settlers and staff who gave of their time in these establishments in cities throughout the country. Many of the young women who resided in the buildings had come from well-to-do families and were students or graduates from one of the so-called Seven Sisters, colleges such as Mount Holyoke, Barnard, and Smith. They sought meaningful work that would bring them out into society and away from the protection of their families, and they were determined to put into practice the concepts they had studied in their philosophy, psychology, and literature classes. This influx of college-educated women into the cities, either as volunteers or paid workers, was a new trend in the social structure of the United States.[2]

The potential for learning from the settlement house experience held great appeal for the settlers, and this, in turn, enriched what the settlement houses were able to offer in their clubs, classes, and other activities. "The 'settlers' found themselves designing and organizing activities to meet the needs of the residents of the neighborhoods in which they were living" (Hansan 2011). Sports-minded residents became coaches, budding teachers taught English, music, and other subjects, and many of them provided leadership for the many adult and children's clubs. "Group purpose developed as members engaged in activities and opened themselves to learning. The club's leader acted as role model, reinforcing ethical and appropriate behavior" (Nadel and Scher 2022, 3). Many settlement house workers from Christodora and other settlements took what they learned and went on to join the new field of social work.

Harry Hopkins

Like many other settlement houses, Christodora House furthered the education of the settlers and launched social activist roles and even careers for some of them. When Christodora House is mentioned in history books and other publications, one name that appears almost without fail is Harry Hopkins.

Hopkins was born in 1890 and grew up in Grinnell, Iowa. He attended Grinnell College, a small private institution, where he majored in history and political science. One of the courses that Hopkins took at Grinnell College that had a deep impression on him was Applied Christianity, with Edward Steiner. Another professor brought Hopkins to work as a counselor in Christodora's camp in New Jersey in the summer of 1912. Christina McColl subsequently offered Hopkins a job as head of boys' activities in New York City. He worked there exclusively until 1913, when he applied for and accepted a position at the Association for Improving the Condition of the Poor (AICP). He continued to live for some time at Christodora House, "working with the boys at the settlement house during the day and for the AICP during the evening" (Hopkins 1999, 61). He met his first wife, Edith Gross, at Christodora House. Edith was a Jewish immigrant from Eastern Europe who came to the settlement house as a young girl and later worked there as a paid staff member. Her duties included overseeing the drama club and serving as secretary to Christina MacColl.

On the Lower East Side of New York, Harry Hopkins was exposed to a type of poverty he had not experienced in his earlier years in Iowa, even though his parents had often struggled to make ends meet on his father's earnings as a harness maker. Living in the Tompkins Square neighborhood, Hopkins experienced firsthand the conditions that the families of the boys he worked with endured, including overcrowded housing, crime, and mistreatment of the neighborhood immigrants by their employers. In Robert Sherwood's account of the relationship between Hopkins and President Franklin D. Roosevelt (FDR), the author remarked that through Harry Hopkin's work as a counselor at Christodora House, he "began to learn of life as it was lived on the Lower East side of New York, which was as complete a sociological laboratory as one could find anywhere on earth" (Sherwood 1948, 22). Some years after his involvement with Christodora House, Hopkins became one of the architects of the New Deal, a comprehensive domestic relief and social reform program in the 1930s, enacted during the Roosevelt administration.

Non-Resident Volunteers

Men and women who volunteered at settlement houses varied in terms of both the amount of time they spent in the physical space and how long their commitment lasted. They oftentimes lived outside the immediate neighborhood, and some had even come to live in New York for the express purpose of working at a settlement house. "The volunteers assumed the burden of leading clubs, soliciting funds, delivering lectures, interceding with other organizations and the public authorities; in the process they learned about the world of the settlement" (Kraus 1980, 132).

There was a constant need to recruit and maintain enough qualified staff to keep Christodora's classes and activities operating. Near the end of the 1902 annual report is a short summary of some of the settlement house's most critical needs. One of these was a call for qualified adults to help with Christodora's programs: "We need more volunteer leaders for clubs and classes. Leaders who are free to set aside one afternoon or evening a week exclusively for Christodora House. We need friends who are interested to support our educational work, contributing to the educational department or to any one specific class" (Christodora House Collection 1902).

Ellen Gould

Ellen Gould was a volunteer from Minnesota who taught immigrants at Christodora House from 1917 to 1919. She was the teacher who corresponded in 1918 with Helen Schechter, an Eastern European immigrant in Gould's English class. An anonymous note that came with the thirty-three letters written by Schechter provided an introduction: "Letters to Ellen T. Gould from Mrs. Helen Schechter whom Nellie taught to speak and write English" (Helen Schechter Letters n.d.).

Because only the letters written by Helen Schechter exist, much of who Ellen Gould was and why she was a volunteer at Christodora have to be inferred from other records and clues. Today she would be described as an English as a Second Language (ESL) teacher. Records from Christodora House list Gould as a part-time volunteer who lived outside the settlement house in the years 1917, 1918, and 1919. Gould then appears in the records in several subsequent years as a financial contributor, but no longer a volunteer worker. In a letter sent from her home in St. Paul, Gould enclosed a donation and expressed how special her time at Christodora had been. She also referred to the fond memories she held for both the settlement house and the people she had encountered there.

PEOPLE IN THE NEIGHBORHOOD

Christodora House was located on the Lower East Side of Manhattan, one of the most densely populated neighborhoods in New York City during the early days of the settlement house movement. "By 1880, over 600,000 New Yorkers lived in 24,000 tenements, each of which housed anywhere from four to several score families" (Yochelson and Czitrom 2007, 20). To put it in relatable terms, "The Lower East Side of 1910 was more than three times as densely populated as New York's most crowded neighborhood [today] even though the predominant five-story tenements of 1910 were only a fraction of the height of today's residential towers" (Anbinder 2016, 359–60). These neighborhoods constituted the world for their inhabitants, and the streets were full of small shops, schools, and places of worship, along with vendors who sold food and other goods from pushcarts and makeshift stalls.

Across from Christodora House and bordering Avenue B was Tompkins Square Park. This was a place where children could play and families escaped the crowded streets and summer heat. Another haven, the Tompkins Square Library, was constructed in 1904 on East Tenth Street between Avenue A and Avenue B, funded by a donation from Andrew Carnegie. In the early days of Christodora House, there was a family-run "shoe repairing and hat cleaning parlor" on the corner of Avenue B and Ninth Street, and the settlement house was only a short walk from the homes of many of the families who came in their free time and used its services. Two individuals who lived nearby and made the best of what Christodora had to offer were Helen Schechter and a boy named Bernard Warach. Although their origins were similar, the lives of these two individuals followed very different trajectories.

Helen Schechter

Helen Schechter and her family were typical of the people in the neighborhood who benefited from Christodora House. A widow with young children, Schechter had come alone to New York in

Figure 4.2. Tompkins Square: Girls fill reading tables on school visit, April 13, 1910. New York Public Library Digital Collections.

1904, when she was only eighteen years old, hopeful that she could earn a living and help her family. She had been born in Tuchów, a city in the region of Galicia that was part of the Austro-Hungarian Empire, and she arrived in the United States at a time when immigrants were coming in unprecedented numbers from Eastern and Southern Europe. Her husband died in 1915 and she was left alone with four children to raise.

Schechter lived on Avenue B and was a devoted mother to her two boys and two girls. She reported in her letters that she often picked up the books that her children brought home from school or the library. She frequently mentioned Christodora House and "Miss MacColl" in her letters to her teacher and related an incident in which she disagreed with the head worker on being able to eat in the summer camp dining hall with her children. Schechter ultimately prevailed, and the incident reveals aspects of both Helen's character and the flexibility and fair-mindedness of Christina MacColl. Helen was a caring person and often expressed concern in her letters for her teacher's health and well-being. She was a staunch advocate for her children and their education and took an active part in deciding where they would attend school and what course of study they would take.[3] The note with the packet of letters to Ellen Gould also included the sentence "Her children, whom she brought up on a Mother's Pension, all made remarkable successes" (Helen Schechter Letters n.d.).

Bernard Warach

Bernard Warach's family, like Helen Schechter's, was Jewish and had Eastern European roots. In his memoir, Warach related stories about his grandparents in Poland and his own childhood growing up in a four-room railroad flat on East Seventh Street between First Avenue and Avenue A. "The street and the apartment house had a diverse population of Jewish, Polish, and Ukrainian immigrants and their American-born children. My father, who came from the Polish Ukraine, could chat in Ukrainian with his neighbors. There was a candy store in our building" (Warach 2011, 33).

Bernard was a member of a boys club that met at Christodora House, and he described the settlement house as "a very congenial center in which to congregate and participate in programs of interest to adolescents. We were in the gymnasium, swimming pool, and social hall every week. We joined a theatre company whose director, Paul Tripp, was an actor on Broadway and a playwright. He was a resident at the settlement house" (41). Warach also spent his summers at Christodora's Northover Camp during junior high school, high school, and while attending City College. "I found my second home at Northover Camp. . . . Northover was unusual in its design and reflected an open philosophy of camping" (53). In Warach's view, this approach to camping and the outdoors was more relaxed than at the other, more regimented summer camps open to New York City children. He held great admiration for the staff, mentioning many by name. He also reflected on the settlement house's ties with Christianity, disclosing that although he did not feel that there was a deliberate attempt to convert the many Catholic and Jewish children who attended the camp, "[t]he experience did wean young people away from the traditions of their families" (54).

Similar to statements made by Henry Hopkins about his experiences at Christodora House, Warach credited the settlement house years as being a pivotal influence on his life:

> Those were the years when my social convictions about the need for change in American society and the possibilities of change effected by social advocacy became fixed. My experience at Christodora House and Northover Camp contributed to my determination to become a social worker. Here was a profession in which I could make a contribution to social change, find a job, and make a living. (55)

Bernard Warach did indeed become a social worker, and he held leadership positions at settlement houses for many years. He was also in service with the government, including a tour overseas as welfare officer in war relief in Germany from 1944 to 1948. Warach considered one of his greatest achievements, documented in detail in his memoir, to be the establishment in 1968 of the Jewish Association for Services for the Aged, which developed into the largest community-based service agency for that population in the United States.

THE WORK

After the initial meeting in 1897, it soon became apparent that the Young Women's Settlement, both in purpose and scope, was only a starting point. The two founders had correctly gauged the need for a settlement house in the Tompkins Square Park neighborhood, but they had miscalculated the extent of the need. "By the end of its first year the membership had to be extended from young women and their mothers to boys because of demand, and in 1898 the name was changed" (Christodora House Collection 1941). A listing in *The Handbook of Settlements* stated that Christodora House was established in order to attend to "the physical, social, intellectual, and spiritual development of the people in the crowded portions of the city of New York, and the training of those who shall be in residence in practical methods of settlement work" (Woods and Kennedy 1911, 235). The neighborhood was one that presented many challenges for the staff:

> Our neighborhood is one that is feverishly ambitious. Restlessly moving up-town and down-town, changing from one business to another, beginning one pursuit and giving it up, hoping to get something better. In such an environment, it has required great determination on the part of the constituency of Christodora House to hold steadily and with intense determination to the essential things which must deepen and enrich every life. (Christodora House Records 1902)

The mobility of the population on the Lower East Side during the late 1800s and early 1900s was due to a variety of factors. In addition to ongoing immigration from abroad and relatives joining one another from within and outside the United States, affordable housing in Manhattan became increasingly scarce. It was usually cheaper to move to Brooklyn or the Bronx if work could be found there. Also, as residents of the Lower East Side became more secure financially, even on a modest level, they were prone to leave the "old neighborhood," a trend that would play out again and again in the history of New York and other cities.

Clubs and Classes

It was common for settlement houses to establish clubs and classes for both children and adults. The clubs served to establish camaraderie among individuals who shared interests or were at the same stage in life, and being a club leader was a good way for settlement house resident workers and volunteers to hone their leadership skills while also sharing these skills and talents. The classes were usually focused on a particular subject or skill, but there was oftentimes an overlap between class and club activities. The clubs at settlement houses were typically smaller than similar groups at some of the other social service agencies, and this helped the leaders bond more closely with club members, especially the children.

> Group membership tended to range from 8–15 and members were homogeneous as to age, geography, gender, and other descriptive characteristics. However, they were often heterogeneous in terms of ability. The adult leader served to identify members with leadership qualities, helped the club establish a constitution, and worked to formulate other administrative functions. (Nadel and Scher 2022, 3)

Throughout the years Christodora House operated, there were many different kinds of clubs, and the newsletters and annual reports are full of descriptions of groups' accomplishments and announcements of new clubs being formed. Christodora differentiated between "junior" and "senior" children, a system that was reflected both in the minimal fees charged as well as club membership age.

Boys and girls at settlement houses more commonly used the physical spaces at different times and were directed to different sports and other activities according to what was deemed appropriate for their gender at the time. For example, while girls had classes in sewing, typing, and dance, boys were likely to be offered carpentry lessons or be taught how to box or play basketball. There were, however, opportunities for boys and girls in the different classes and clubs to intermingle for events like debates, entertainment by guest artists and performers, and interclub socials, all of which "helped to create a fine social spirit" (Christodora House Collection 1915).

The Mothers' Club, one of the many clubs created for parents, was documented extensively in the Christodora House records. Minutes were kept for this club and mention of it appeared in many of the reports over the years. In the 1915 account of the year's activities, for example, there was a disclaimer that the Mothers' Club had not been as active recently as some of the others, but the author insisted that this did not reflect lack of interest on the members' part. On the contrary, the members of the Mothers' Club had been engaged in a valuable endeavor that brought them into contact with their peers throughout the city:

> Being affiliated with the Mothers' Clubs of New York City brings us in touch with other people and what has been done for the betterment not only of our neighborhood, but the entire city. Such measures as "Widowed Mothers' Pension Bill," "Moving Picture Censorship," "High Cost of Living," and "Minimum Wage," etc. have all come up for consideration and approval.

> The reports of our delegates have been very interesting and it
> is encouraging to see what can be accomplished by joining
> together and making a united effort for a common cause.
> (Christodora House Collection 1915)

The list of topics illustrates some of the vital concerns of families at the time as well as how settlement house clubs connected women across the city with one another.

Younger members of clubs at the settlement house were also provided an opportunity to explore the world outside the neighborhood. There is a photograph of a dozen young boys standing on the deck of a ferryboat with their chaperone behind them. Below the photo, a description of the club to which they all belonged reads "The Citizens Club is composed of boys from 12 to 14 years of age. During the winter special study was given to places of interest in Greater New York. In the spring and summer many of these places were visited, car fares being paid out of the club treasury" (Christodora House Collection 1902). It is likely that most of these boys would not have otherwise been able to afford to venture beyond the blocks in which they lived and attended school (and for some where they also worked), and so these club field trips opened up the world to them.

Settlement houses also offered a wide variety of classes for adults and children in the neighborhood. The subject matter decided upon for the first members of the Young Women's Settlement were millinery, typewriting, dressmaking, English, and stenography. After that, classes were continually added over the years. These included carpentry, clay modeling, first aid, stage design, early childhood development, and vocal training, among many others. Individual tutoring was also available for those who were interested in taking civil service or college entrance examinations. During a time when the public school system was overwhelmed with large numbers of students, many of whom were still learning English, the instruction provided by Christodora supplemented the school curriculum and provided more personalized instruction and attention. In addition, some of the classes focused on subject matter in which school-age and older patrons were interested but to which they would otherwise have had little or no exposure.

Over the decades, one of the most popular divisions within Christodora House was the music school, where students could learn to play instruments, sing, or just learn to listen to and appreciate different types of music. Christodora's music school was a member of the Association of Music School Settlements, but unlike those settlement houses that focused exclusively on music, Christodora House offered many subject areas students could choose from. In contrast, the Third Street Music School Settlement, established in 1894, focused exclusively on music, and it is still thriving on East Eleventh Street in New York.

Religion and Christodora House

In the book *Settlement Folk,* Mina Carson stated, "There were many shades of opinion concerning religion in the settlement" (Carson 1990, 57). The role of the Social Gospel in the settlement house movement, both in England and the United States, has been discussed in a previous chapter, and I also pointed out earlier that Christodora House was seen by some outsiders as less secular than other settlement houses, even though it was officially nonsectarian. "Non-sectarianism, or at the very least, non-denominationalism, was for settlement workers one of the key differences between their institutions and the inner-city missions run by various Christian sects" (James 2001, 60).

Over the course of the past several years, I have read many accounts of individual settlement houses and the settlement house movement, and have spent many hours in Columbia University's library examining Christodora House correspondence and other records. It is clear to me from my research that there were a number of Christian activities and traditions at Christodora that were not part of the routine at other settlement houses. This was especially true from 1897 to the mid-1930s, the years when Christina MacColl was head worker. These activities likely contributed to Christodora House's being included, along with ten other New York City settlement houses, in a list of "New York City Neighborhood Houses Maintaining Religious Instruction." The activities included "a children's hour, Sunday afternoon service, Bible classes, men's meetings, [and] week day studies in religion, etc." (Woods and Kennedy 1911, 235).

The meetings and scheduling at Christodora House that included religion-related themes, at least in the early years, were a well-known part of the life of that settlement house. Christodora, however, has always been classified as nonsectarian because it was not officially allied to a specific religion or denomination. To my mind, the best description of the role that religion and religious beliefs played at Christodora House came from Christina MacColl herself:

> Enough of God's love can make Catholic and Protestant, Jew and Gentile live in harmony, each expressing the religious belief which he daily learns from God. The settlement ever seeks to emphasize the common grounds, never to emphasize differences. The common ground of our religious life is the fatherhood and love of God. Can we help every boy or girl, man or woman with whom we come into contact, to realize in a practical way in the things of everyday life, God's real presence,

tender love and ever-present strength and comfort according
to the need? Do you see how far this is from what is commonly
known as proselytizing? (MacColl 1903).

More about the role of religion at Christodora House and in the
settlement house movement in general is featured in the final
section of this book.

CHRISTODORA HOUSE AND THE ARTS

Christodora House, in addition to housing a music school and
offering lessons in art and drama to patrons of all ages, was a
center for cultural activities by artists and writers who later
became well known nationally and internationally. The workers at Christodora, along with other individuals who supported
the work of the settlement house, were responsible for creating
organizations, introducing programs, and otherwise contributing in valuable ways not only to the organization but also to the
cultural life of New York City and the nation. Both in the building at 147 Avenue B at the turn of the twentieth century and
when the larger structure at 143 Avenue B was built in 1928,
music, literature, and drama were important contributions of
the settlement house to the neighborhood. New York City
attracted a wide array of singers, songwriters, playwrights, poets,
novelists, actors, and musicians, and members of the public often
donated tickets to performances to Christodora, which were
then distributed to children and their families.

Dugald Stewart Walker was a book illustrator in the early
1900s; his work appeared in fairy tales and other kinds of books.
After working in the theater with producer David Belasco,
Walker brought his talents to Christodora House in its early
years and premiered his experimental Portmanteau Theatre,

which would later become a traveling repertory company. As reported years later in a Christodora report: "Stewart Walker's famous experiment of the Portmanteau Theatre—which had to be abandoned during the [First World War] on account of railway transportation difficulties—had its first productions at Christodora House. A big gymnasium gave ample scope for what he wanted to do and he benefitted much by the opportunity afforded him" (Christodora House Collection 1935).

Also receiving his start at Christodora House was George Gershwin, who performed his first piano recital in 1914, when he was sixteen years old. George's brother Ira Gershwin was a member of the Finley Club, a literary society at Christodora, and the entertainment for the evening of March 21, 1914, was expressly for members of that club. In addition to George's solo piano performance of a work he had written specifically for the evening, the program also featured vocal selections by George Gershwin and Charles Rose (Christodora House Collection 1914). George Gershwin went on to became a renowned composer and pianist who worked in both the popular and classical musical genres. Ira Gershwin, who became a Pulitzer Prize–winning lyricist, often collaborated on musical compositions with his younger brother George.

The Poets' Guild

The Poets' Guild at Christodora House was a unique organization that enriched the cultural life of the Lower East Side and New York City as a whole. It was established by Anna Hempstead Branch, a Smith College graduate and longtime volunteer and occasional resident at Christodora. Her activities as a volunteer "included reading verse to migrant women and children and encouraging them to write their own poems" (Rubin 2007, 184).

Anna Branch had begun volunteering at Christodora several years before she started the Poets' Guild in 1920.[4] In an illustrated brochure published shortly after it was established, there were twenty-three poets associated with the Guild, "representative American poets, banded together not for their mutual inspiration but for the encouragement of the young people of the East Side tenements who possess the poetic instinct" (Christodora House Collection 1922).

The Poets' Guild at Christodora House sponsored writing classes, organized writing groups, and encouraged participants to read poetry and utilize it as a means of personal expression. Branch was an energetic proponent of the arts and initially approached poets whom she deemed might be interested in the idea and practice of social service; she said about the Poets' Guild that "its central feature was that poets would act as 'councillors' to the settlement's youth clubs" (Rubin 2007, 287). Margaret Widdemer, a poet and one of these mentors, described her own approach toward the art of poetry: "My aesthetic bias has always been towards the classic and conservative; curiously mingled with a deep interest in social problems" (Bucks County Artists Database). Branch also enlisted Dugald Stewart Walker, the same person who originated the Portmanteau Theatre, to design the Poets' Guild logo, a candlelit winged torch.

"The Unbound Anthology"

Anna Branch attracted talented poets to read their work and hold discussions about poetry at Christodora House. These authors included Robert Frost, Sara Teasdale, Carl Sandburg, and Josephine Preston Peabody, to name only a few. In order to ensure that poetry in printed form was affordable for everyone,

Figure 4.3. Poets' Guild Room, Christodora House, ca. 1929. Photo by Samuel H. Gottscho (1875–1971), Christodora House Collection, Rare Book and Manuscript Library, Columbia University.

the Poets' Guild produced what they called "The Unbound Anthology." Selected poems from contemporary authors as well as from American and British literature were printed on individual sheets of paper and made available to the public. Patrons, including schools and clubs, could choose the poems they wanted in loose-leaf form for as little as five cents each to form a collection that was individualized according to the reader's preference.

The low price was feasible because the strategy of keeping the sheets unbound circumvented several of the costs of republication in book form. The difference between loose-leaf and bound pages not only did away with the expense of binding, but also convinced most authors and publishers to waive the usual permission fees charged for reprinting. Out of support for the project's social service agenda, authors also agreed to forgo any

income from sales; all revenue went back to the Guild to fund
additions to the "anthology" (Rubin 2007, 188–89).

The Poets' Guild was active well into the 1930s, "and by 1935
included a twenty-member speaking choir [and] some of its
classes carried university extension credit from New York University" (191). Anna Hempstead Branch's contribution to poetry
in the United States was significant because she was able to
attract both famous and unknown poets to a neighborhood
organization and, as a result, assure greater access to that genre.
"Within a few years she had become the most prominent advocate among early-twentieth century settlement house workers
of poetry's centrality to the nation's welfare, and particularly its
utility in meeting the educational and spiritual needs of urban
immigrants" (184).

RECREATION, PLAY, AND THE OUTDOORS

The settlement house movement was also allied with the public
playground and park movement, which advocated for outdoor
places in the city where children could be children. Christodora
House provided safe recreational and outdoor experiences to
families both in New York City and at Northover Camp in New
Jersey. The counselors and administrators of Northover provided visitors with a healthy environment along with opportunities to learn and grow that complemented and enhanced the
Christodora programs in Manhattan. The structure at 147 Avenue B, however, was not adequate for the number of participants
and range of athletic and outdoor activities the settlement
wanted to offer. To compensate, Christodora cooperated with
other locations, such as St. Mark's Chapel, the Madison Square
Church House, and Hamilton Fish Park, all of which made their

own facilities available to the settlement (Christodora House Collection 1915). The Christodora children and their instructors and coaches were able to make use of those other venues for sports and practice sessions, but even those arrangements did not meet the demand. It was widely acknowledged that recreation was a crucial need for younger members of the settlement house, and when the building at 143 Avenue B was built in 1928, some of the most cherished and well-used features were the pool and gymnasium.

Christodora's Northover Camp was forty miles and a world away from the densely populated Lower East Side. "In 1907, 72 acres of wooded hillside at Bound Brook, New Jersey were acquired as a country camp" (Christodora House Collection 1935). The land was a gift from Mr. George La Monte, the owner of a family paper company. The camp, which later expanded to over ninety acres, developed its capacity over the years and hosted picnics, day trips, and occasional staff training and meetings. However, the camp's primary goal was to provide a place where children and their parents could come for a vacation in the country for days or weeks at a time.

After the camp was established, the Christodora House constitution added this objective: "For boarding or keeping during the Summer months, of children from the crowded portions of the great cities of the United States and especially the City of New York" (Christodora House Collection 1908). Christina MacColl was responsible for the physical building and activities in the city and the camp facilities, staff, and programming, which she coordinated with a camp director. Together, the two locales offered children in New York City and some of their adult family members a chance to escape the heat and congestion of the urban environment for varying lengths of time. More significantly, it provided all of the participants, but particularly those with asthma or other breathing disorders, relief from the pollution of the city. They were also fed nutritious food from the camp's own gardens or nearby farms. The camp grew from a group of tents its first year to a collection of central and residential buildings and outdoor facilities that welcomed hundreds of visitors every year.

PHYSICAL LOCATIONS

Christodora performed its work as a settlement house in a number of places in New York City between 1897 and the 1960s. From 1897 to 1898, it was located at 163 Avenue B and was known as the Young Women's Settlement. In 1898, the settlement moved to 147 Avenue B. This was necessary since, as the head worker remarked, "Our numbers had outgrown our rooms" (MacColl 1933). In addition to a change of location, the name changed from the Young Women's Settlement to Christodora House. The official address from that point and until 1928 was 147 Avenue B, even after a major renovation, completed in 1912, when the buildings at 145 and 147 were combined.

However, the building most associated with Christodora House is the one inscribed with its name, which still stands at the corner of Avenue B and Ninth Street, across from Tompkins Square Park. Referred to by some as "the skyscraper settlement," the building at 143 Avenue B was a symbol at first of the work of the settlement house, later becoming emblematic of worsening socioeconomic conditions, and, still later, of neighborhood gentrification. Arthur Curtiss James and his wife, Harriet, had provided the financing for the building at 143 Avenue B, dedicated in 1928. The plans for the construction of the building, to be designed by architect Henry Pelton, were outlined in a Christodora House board meeting on February 14:

> The first step . . . was the purchase of the corner lot at Ninth
> Street and Avenue B thus giving a lot 69 feet on Avenue B and
> 93 feet on Ninth Street. On this lot it is Mrs. James' plan to build
> a building adequate to house the needs of Christodora House
> for the next twenty-five years and in addition produce an income
> sufficient to pay the operating expenses of the Christodora
> House work. To do that it will be necessary to tear down all
> the existing buildings and put up a modern fireproof building.
> (Christodora House Collection 1927)

The existing buildings referred to here are the ones combined in 1912—namely, 145 and 147 Avenue B—as well as the
one purchased on Ninth Street, which was located directly
behind the Avenue B structures.

The building constructed in 1928 had two distinct uses. The
first five stories in the lower part were for the use of the settlement house and general public and contained the concert hall
and studios of the music school. There were also workshops, club
rooms, and classrooms for both adults and children. The lower
floors also served the public by way of the house's clinic and
dietary kitchens, and there was a pool and gymnasium. In order
to help fund the work of the settlement house, the top nine floors
of Christodora House housed what was called the "Club Residence." In addition to providing living space for 150 men and
women, there were amenities such as a lounge, library, and dining room. A roof garden and solarium were also provided for
the use of the club residents. "Although the rental accommodation was cheaper than elsewhere in the city, it was too expensive
for the tenement-dwelling 'neighbors' of Christodora House. The
affordable housing was targeted at a different group of men
and women, from beyond the Lower East Side, who would live
in the settlement as 'guests' rather than 'neighbors' or resident

Figure 4.4. Music auditorium, Christodora House. Photo February 11, 1929, by Samuel H. Gottscho (1875–1971), Museum of the City of New York.

Figure 4.5. General view of the dining room, Christodora House. Photo February 5, 1929, by Samuel H. Gottscho (1875–1971), Museum of the City of New York.

workers" (Blunt 2008, 562). In 1933, Christina MacColl told her audience, "I hate to have you think Christodora House has always been a skyscraper. It wasn't at all. It lay its roots very deep before it reached skyward."

Alison Blunt's 2008 article, what she terms a "house biography" of Christodora House, described in depth the dual purpose of the building as a settlement house and residence for more than just the workers. She proposed that a residence of the kind incorporated into the new building at 143 Avenue B represented an alternative model for urban housing. However, it was not meant as a residence for the local population, which was decidedly in need of additional and more affordable housing options, but, rather, was intended to draw new people to live in the area:

> Whilst the presence of such "guests" was deemed necessary to provide a regular income and potential volunteers for the settlement house, their relocation to Tompkins Square, and the nature of their accommodation, should also be situated in the wider context of early public housing schemes which "resembled middle-income redevelopments" and sought to attract other New Yorkers, particularly those working in the adjacent financial district, to live on the Lower East Side. (562)

A similar enticement, but this time to affluent New Yorkers, would later be extended to another generation and eventually lead to struggles over real estate speculation, dislocation, and gentrification. The Christodora settlement house carried on with its work at 143 Avenue B between 1928 and 1948, at which point the building became the property of the city of New York. The reasons for the move, the legal battles in which the settlement house was involved, and the options for the settlement's next location all demonstrate the tenacity of Christodora's board members and its attorneys, and the organization's deep

Figure 4.6. Children and bus outside Christodora House, 147 Avenue B. Christodora House Records, Rare Book and Manuscript Library, Columbia University.

connection with the neighborhood. In a 1947 newspaper article entitled "City to Get Settlement," Christodora House director Herbert Biele optimistically predicted that "the community services of that organization would continue without undue hardship in the present building until spring, and later in a new building" (*New York Times* 1947). In the end, however, it was a difficult and often contentious transition. Events in the years leading up to the surrender of the building are detailed in the following pages, culminating with the years of 1947 and 1948, which led to the sale of the building on Avenue B to the city of New York and the relocation of Christodora House.

PRACTICAL IDEALISM

Christina MacColl and the other settlement house leaders combined the qualities of practicality and idealism in their

planning and work. Given the limited resources of Christodora House in any one year, the workers aimed at meeting the
most urgent needs of the community as they arose, in addition
to what they normally did. For example, during the World War
I years, staff at the settlement rolled bandages and knit clothing
for servicemen abroad, held war-bond drives, treated victims
of the influenza epidemic, and provided low-cost medical and
dental care for the neighbors. Likewise, during the Depression,
Christodora helped many of those in the neighborhood who
were unemployed by distributing food to the families or helping the adults find jobs.

It was also important for settlement houses to avoid dupli-
cating services that other individuals, groups, and agencies made
available. This required an awareness of what was going on in
the neighborhood and listening carefully to the adults and
children who came through their doors. As MacColl put it, "All
work in a Settlement must be tentative. Here we introduce sewing classes for children when sewing is not being taught in the
public schools. As soon as all of our children in the public schools
have something, we can drop it in our settlement" (MacColl
1903). Recognizing the need for books and other reading material to be freely available in the neighborhood, the cofounders
had included a reading room in their limited space at 163 Avenue B during the first year of operation. After the move a year
later, they made books accessible, especially in light of the growing membership. A few years later, however, the need lessened:

> We have had a small library at Christodora House because we
> find that our young people had not the time or would not take
> the trouble to consult the public libraries located at some dis-
> tance. One of the New York City-Carnegie-libraries is being
> erected on Tenth Street near the corner of Avenue B. I am

> hoping this will enable us to give up our circulating library keep-
> ing only a few of the books necessary with our club and educa-
> tional work. (MacColl 1903)

Providing only what the neighbors could not get elsewhere was also one of the likely reasons Christodora was forced to close its music school in 1936, and at one point the settlement's health and dental clinics were cut back. This did not mean that offering music classes and health services meant any less to the workers at Christodora House, only that they knew these things were already being taken care of by other settlement houses or social service agencies.

An important principle of social settlements was, and continues to be, respect and consideration for the neighbors' needs and strengths. Contrary to accounts that settlement houses pursued their own agendas over those of their neighbors, there is ample evidence in the Christodora House records that the house workers valued the contributions that those from outside could provide. Just as each settlement house was unique, so was its relationship with the neighborhood and how it handled different situations. Sometimes the settlement house needed to take the lead—for example, in terms of how the facility would be used—and sometimes the responsibility rested with other community members. In the same 1903 letter from which the examples above were drawn, MacColl explained the settlement house's way of handling matters better left to the people of the neighborhood:

> It has become the policy of the House not to appear to take the
> lead aggressively in initiating new movements. Wherever possi-
> ble, the need has been planted by some natural leader in the
> community, so that as far as possible changes might spring
> even more, as it were, from the local soil, than if they had been

fostered in the Settlement. Thus a member of the Alumni Association was encouraged to take the steps which brought about the placing of a wading pool in Tompkins Square. (MacColl 1903)

CHANGE ON THE HORIZON: THE 1930s AND 1940s

Not everyone agrees on the time span of the original model of the settlement house, at least in terms of its goals and whether the workers needed to reside on-site. Allen Davis proposed that, in terms of the original settlement house model, "World War I marked the end of an era" (1967, xiii). Others place the end point of the worker-in-residence/social service–providing settlement house and catalyst for reform as continuing into the 1920s. Davis elaborated: "For, while they continued to work for reform throughout the war, and on a limited basis during the 1920s and after, the spirit was different and their movement had changed" (xiii).

Marking 1920 as a turning point makes sense for several reasons. First of all, legislation was limiting immigration to the United States. In addition, compared with earlier years, "schools and other public agencies took over many successful programs such as Americanization classes, kindergartens, and playgrounds" (Trolander 1975, 15). And then came the Great Depression in 1929. The settlement houses turned some of their focus on functions like employment and direct monetary relief, which, to a great degree, were beyond what they were accustomed to handling. The Works Progress Administration (WPA) relief program under President Franklin D. Roosevelt (with the assistance of Harry Hopkins) was a godsend when it came into being but then left a huge hole when it suddenly ended. "The WPA program was of major concern to the settlements after its organization in June 1935, both because some of its projects helped bolster the settlements' programs and because the WPA took on many settlement neighbors" (Trolander 1975, 80). This concern deepened when the government canceled the WPA and pulled government support for workers who had become important, if not invaluable, to settlement houses. Christodora House had also benefited from the earlier Federal Emergency Relief Administration (FERA) program in 1934, when the settlement house was chosen as the location for New York City's first federally financed "emergency nursery school," the first of twenty-five that were planned for the city (*New York Times* 1934).

In 1942, Herbert Biele, director of Christodora House, wrote an extensive and insightful report that reviewed the state of affairs at Christodora for the years 1941 and 1942. "In general, the usual program of Settlement activities obtained throughout the year: clubs, physical education, crafts, dramatics, health and dental services, personal guidance, the camping seasons, outdoor picnics, field days, trips to the museums, and associated projects with other organizations" (Christodora House Collection 1942). He then reported on the needs of the neighborhood, the supply of personnel at Christodora, and, finally, the financial aspect of running a settlement. The war, which the United States joined in 1941, was a game changer in Biele's view: "The settlement program had just about reached the peak of its effectiveness, when our entry into the war upset all lesser plans. Casual interest in helping our friends overseas became a feverish desire to do something concrete and immediate." The director went on to describe some of the cuts in financial support that had affected Christodora the most:

Along normal lines, arrangements were made to have the Federal Music [P]roject return to our building. Hardly had it become re-established than all such projects were cancelled by orders from Washington. Similarly, the WPA Adult Education classes were withdrawn; and although the staff of the Settlement extended itself to offset those losses, no great progress was made. At this writing, this particular need is lessened, for other affairs claim the attention of those who usually would attend those classes.

This illustrates the extent to which adjustments had to be made at Christodora House to allow for what was happening in the country and in the world. At the same time, the settlement house's facilities were, as usual, shared with a wide range of other agencies, including the Boys Club, Stuyvesant High School, the Jewish Board of Guardians, the Parent-Teacher Association, and the Civilian Defense Council. Each of these different entities "conducted activities of its own as well as having its enrollees participate in our affairs. This 'open door policy' necessitated considerable readjustment of the Settlement's originally planned program, but resulted in cumulative good to the neighborhood at large."

The director's report included details about the occupancy of the residence and is, in retrospect, an indication of what was to come.

General occupancy ran higher later this year than for the corresponding period a year previous, but still lagged behind the high record of several years ago. Contacts were made, and are being pursued, to discover the possibilities of having the House designated as an official stopping place for military or other government personnel. While no substantial progress was made, we were able to attract individual workers in some of the civilian offices that have recently shifted from Washington to New

York. Our location discourages many. (Christodora House
Collection 1942)

Because more than half of the sixteen-story Christodora building was devoted to the residence, having empty rooms or floors
was a problem, and as a result the board actively sought tenants
who did not match the original plan for the residential space.

The records for 1934 had indicated that forty thousand dollars needed to be raised to meet the settlement house's expenses,
and a flyer in 1935 stated, "All told, income from settlement
members this past year paid 20 percent of the actual cost of
activities for them." Seven years later, in 1942, Director Biele predicted that the following year's budget (1942–1943) would likely
entail a deficit of a little over fifty thousand dollars. Neverthe-
less, the director was hopeful for the future and looked at the
big picture: "The situation is a challenge to be met—for war or
no war (or possibly because of the war) the work of the Settlement House is assuming an importance and a substantiality
equal to any it ever before had."

TURNING POINT

A report by the Christodora Foundation written in the mid-
1980s looked back at how Christodora House was able to attain
its early goals and aspirations:

> The settlement house had originally been established to provide
> unified cultural, professional, and recreational exchange within
> an underprivileged immigrant community. Offering all the best
> health and cultural services which the members could not have
> afforded, Christodora House was at that time a utopian dream—
> and it worked, for a while. (Christodora Inc.1986).

The optimism expressed by Director Herbert Biele in 1942 could only be sustained for a few more years. The Friends Service Committee rented one entire floor of the 143 Avenue B building, and other changes were proposed to keep the settlement house afloat financially. However, the Executive Committee and the director finally decided that the best option was to sell the building. In an April 1947 letter to the board members, Biele stated, "Nineteen years of operation in the present building have demonstrated that a combination of a Club Residence with a Settlement House in a building of such size cannot be made to fulfill the purposes originally intended" (Christodora House Collection 1947). The relatively remote location of Christodora House, something Biele had referred to in an earlier report, combined with the logistical difficulties proved to be too much. In the same letter, he explained: "The combination of the two diverse activities under one management causes a corresponding diversion of thinking and planning which is detrimental to the best operation of either the Settlement or the Club Residence."

After considerable negotiation with the city of New York, the building was finally sold to the city for over $1.5 million on the basis of the right of eminent domain.[5] The city intended to use the building for an existing program for juveniles currently being housed elsewhere, and the building was never used to house a settlement again. In her account of the building at 143 Avenue B, Blunt concluded: "As a skyscraper built for settlement work, Christodora House represented a new, but ultimately unsuccessful form of dwelling in the city" (2008, 550).

CONCLUSION

Was the inability to work out of a particular address or building the only measuring stick by which the success of

Christodora or, for that matter, any settlement house, can be gauged? During the twenty years that Christodora House was based at 143 Avenue B, drawing on decades of prior experience and a solid reputation in the neighborhood, staff were able to welcome thousands of individuals through their doors, year after year. As settlement staff had for years, they taught classes, supervised sports, conducted clinics, led clubs for adults and children, and helped foster a genuine sense of community. They also sponsored nationally respected arts programs and brought in authors, actors, directors, and musicians to teach and perform.

For three more decades, from 1948 to the late 1970s, Christodora House continued to operate as a social settlement that provided clubs, instruction, and other activities to New Yorkers in public housing and the surrounding neighborhood. As will be described in the next chapter, the rooms at the Riis Houses and in the building Christodora House purchased on First Street in 1956 were places where people could come together, learn, and grow. Through Christodora programs both within and outside the city, adults and children could also enjoy and learn to appreciate nature and the outdoors. Christodora, as a nonprofit organization but no longer a settlement house, still exists today, working with and on behalf of New York City youth, who are afforded academic, wilderness, and other experiences that make them stronger individuals and community members.

Christodora House was more than just a building. Like other settlement houses, it came into being during a time before the government had established comprehensive social programs for the poor. Settlement houses joined other social service organizations in New York City that were able to effect lasting social and political change, starting at the local level. The work of the settlement house arose from the needs of the neighbors, and the results were intended to benefit all, including the residents. The impact that Christina MacColl, in particular, had on Christodora House and on everyone associated with it cannot be overstated. MacColl exemplified the contributions women have made to the labors and overall ethos of the settlement house. She was the heart of Christodora House, working there and providing leadership as head worker from the house's founding in 1897 until 1935. MacColl died in 1939, and upon hearing of her death, William Krampner, principal of a school on the Lower East Side, wrote this to his students:

> One of Miss MacColl's aims was to make Christodora House a place where children may always be happy. Not only are children and grown-ups made happy in Christodora House, but their lives are enriched there. Miss MacColl was a marvelous builder, a builder of souls. The bricks with which she built were thousands of human beings . . . How well she built may be attested by the accomplishments of the thousands of graduates of Christodora House, and by the great esteem in which she is held by all in this neighborhood. (Christodora House Collection 1940)

In an essay in memory of Christina MacColl, the author says that Miss MacColl once told a young applicant, "Your first and chief qualification must be that you have a heart large enough to admit everyone" (Christodora House Collection 1939). Based on the outpouring of gratitude during her life and the many expressions of grief and appreciation upon her death, it is clear that MacColl embodied the kind of acceptance and open heart that were expected of all the settlement house workers.

In the years following World War I and then after World War II, New York City and the country experienced cataclysmic changes that affected everyone in the nation in all walks of life. Urban residents, particular those who were poor, struggled to find affordable and safe housing and jobs that paid a living wage—many of the same issues immigrants and other city dwellers had endured in past decades. Some of the settlement house work continued in the same or new locations, while other settlement services were taken over by government agencies, private foundations, and numerous other organizations. But there is no disputing that Christodora and the other settlement houses in New York and across the country succeeded in planting some vital seeds, and that there was still work to be done.

5

COMING DOWN TO EARTH

Christodora House After 1948

AT THIS POINT IN the chronicle of Christodora House, it is necessary to distinguish between the work and the building. In a sense, they went their separate ways. The social services and community outreach relocated to the Riis Houses in 1948, and the building on Avenue B, originally intended to house a New York City facility for juveniles, was underutilized and then languished for decades before being converted into condominium apartments. The initial focus in this chapter is on the settlement work that continued in new locations and at Northover Camp. Following that is an account of what happened to the building when it was no longer a settlement house, placing it in the context of events that unfolded in the neighborhood.

In the years after World War II, settlement houses and private social work agencies entered into partnerships with new public housing developments. Settlement houses in particular have had a long history of working in urban neighborhoods and advocating for the local residents and, as such, have been an important resource and partner. Public housing in New York City started on a relatively small scale in 1934 to combat the housing crisis caused by the Great Depression. By the 1960s, there were nearly seventy public housing projects in the city, containing over one thousand units (Ferré-Sadurní 2018). When Christodora moved to the Jacob Riis Houses, the housing project on Avenue D was brand-new, having just been completed on January 17, 1949.

Once the transition from the building on Avenue B was made, it was time for those associated with Christodora House to adjust to their new location. Working within a public housing project and specifically at the Jacob Riis Houses had its advantages. First of all, the location was still on the Lower East Side and many of the families who utilized Christodora's services could attend club meetings and participate in other activities right where they lived. Second, Christodora did not have to pay rent and utilities for the space they used at the Riis Houses. Finally, the five-year contract that Christodora signed with the New York City Housing Authority (NYCHA)—the terms of the contract effective as of October 1948—stated that either party could terminate the agreement with ninety days' notice.

The disadvantage of operating on public housing premises was largely due to greater involvement by outsiders in the settlement house's efforts, particularly in terms of governmental financing and reporting requirements. The socially oriented work in which Christodora had been engaged since 1897 had depended mostly on money and property supplied by wealthy donors, although a small amount was also collected every year in membership fees and in renting out some of the facilities to other organizations. Due to these private funding arrangements, the settlement had been largely free (subject to approval by the board) to plan and adjust its own programs and direction. In the post–World War II years, social services were becoming more compartmentalized and had been increasingly relegated to specialists and separate departments. "The settlements changed from being informal organizations oriented to service provision and community building, in which funding was a highly private matter, to formalized, multiservice agencies dependent on contracted public funds for categorical programs" (Fisher and Fabricant 2002, 3).

There was also a significant difference between the philosophy underlying Christodora's work and the beliefs and practices that were becoming the norm in professional social work and health and mental services, particularly when these were dependent on government funding. While the overall tone and relationships at Christodora House had in the past been neighborly and relatively informal, the kind of social work that emerged after the peak of the settlement house era was often framed in terms of a client-provider relationship. In addition, government-funded programs frequently had specific goals in mind or were aimed at a targeted population. This became more and more apparent to Christodora staff as time went on.

What follows is a description of the ways in which Christodora House carried on with its work in the new setting, with a focus on both what was going well and on difficulties encountered along the way. Ultimately, a decision would be made that was aimed at holding to core settlement house values, which resulted in major changes for Christodora House.

REPORTS FROM THE FIELD (1950—1956)

Christodora was not alone in the move from its own building to one of the city's public housing projects. According to a 1950 newspaper article, "At present a dozen settlement houses have either moved bodily into public housing developments or used their experienced staffs to establish programs there." Others were soon to follow. The person cited in the article was Helen Harris, executive director of United Neighborhood Houses (UNH), the coordinating agency that at the time represented a total of fifty-three area settlement houses (*New York Times* 1950). As of 2022, over seventy years later, UNH was still working with forty-five settlement houses in New York City (United Neighborhood Houses).

Reading Christodora House annual reports from 1949 through 1956, one gets a sense that the work of the settlement house was going relatively well and that the workers and directors were meeting many of their goals. There was occasional mention of what could be called "adjustment pains," but this was nothing new to the Christodora staff and board members. As had been true throughout their history, they needed to be flexible and responsive to current circumstances and remain open to changing course, sometimes abruptly, as needed. These reports illustrate the significant numbers of community members that the settlement house served as well as a lack of fit between what the settlement accomplished on a day-to-day basis in the public housing setting and what the perceived needs were on the part of the NYCHA. Also, starting right away with the 1949–1950 report, there were remarks that the facilities on Avenue D were neither adequate nor "permanently acceptable" for Christodora House's purposes. That theme was repeated the following year with the news that a search was under way to find an affordable property that could accommodate both present and future planned activities. In particular, the settlement wanted to be able to establish a full-time day-care center, reestablish health and dental clinics, and provide expanded family services.

The annual reports from this time consisted for the most part of factual summaries and statistics that showed the strength of the settlement house's enrollment and breadth of activities, both in the city and at Northover Camp in New Jersey. About half of each year's report was devoted to an account of how existing resources and financial assets, including investments, were being put to use. The rest of each report specified the number of members and participants that were served in the city and at Northover Camp and how many of these were registered with Christodora House. There was also a paragraph or two about who was on staff and which positions they filled that year, as well as details of the activities being conducted, with special mention of new or discontinued programs. The reports also described the progress being made and any problems the organization was facing that year or had solved.

Who Came Through the Doors?

The annual reports differentiated between "enrolled members" of the settlement house and other participants. It is clear from reading the reports that the members made up only a fraction of the adults and children who participated in activities and benefited from services in the rooms at the Riis Houses that were used for Christodora House activities. Starting in the 1949–1950 fiscal year and ending in 1955–1956, an average of 954 members were considered regular or settlement house members. An early report from the initial years in public housing stated that about half of these came from the Riis Houses, while the remainder lived in what it referred to as "the outer neighborhood."

The lowest number of members from the seven-year span of annual reports was 667 in the year that ended in 1951, and the highest was 1,359 members in fiscal year 1955–1956. It is important to note that in October 1955, Christodora House signed a lease (with an option to buy) to use space in the buildings at 84 and 86 First Street, which had housed the Recreation Rooms and Settlement, a Jewish settlement house. This gave Christodora House more space for activities and administrative offices; it gained full occupancy of the buildings in October 1956 and later purchased them. The facilities on First Street contained a gymnasium and auditorium, both of which had been sorely missed since the move from Avenue B in 1948.[1]

The reports did not typically contain spreadsheets or tables with the numbers of participants clearly listed, so it was often difficult to get an accurate tally of adults and children who came to the Riis Houses on Avenue D or made the trip to the camp in New Jersey. In addition, some of the numbers were expressed in terms of "attendances" or "contacts" and not discrete numbers of individuals. However, it was clear that there was a great demand on the settlement's services, especially when large number of Puerto Rican families moved to New York in the 1950s. This changed not only the number of program participants and neighborhood residents but also the age and language demographic. This excerpt from the 1953–1954 annual report is a good example of how these details were presented, keeping in mind that the number of registered members that year was 819:

In 1953–54 total settlement attendances were over 42,000, which included 305 contacts made by a Spanish-speaking staff member on newly arrived Puerto Rican families; 189 health, budget, and homemaking conferences by the nurse, some 300 home visits, office interviews and personal consultations by the program director. In all, some 3,300 people used our facilities or benefited from our services. (Christodora House Collection 1954)

What Did They Do?

The normal types of settlement house classes and clubs continued when Christodora moved to the Riis Houses and then, a few years later, when the settlement was able to expand to the First Street premises. The reports identified such varied classes as crafts, music, homemaking, hygiene, sewing, woodwork, dramatics, and Scouts. In addition to regularly scheduled activities, there were also less formal groups and activities that made use of the game rooms and lounges and attended social dances. At one point, weekend dances for teens were held on Saturday and Sunday evenings, but these were discontinued when the crowds overwhelmed the space. In addition, there were simply not enough personnel available to oversee the dances, and the noise disturbed some of the tenants. However, it was also reported that "to some extent this loss is offset by similar activities in the First Street buildings" (Christodora House Collection 1956). The settlement house also continued to sponsor special holiday gatherings as well as trips to local points of interest, and to places and events such as zoos, baseball games, and the circus.

In 1951, a Summer Play Center in the city was established at the Riis Houses, and 150 children were enrolled for games, trips, a story hour, and other activities. In 1954, in addition to the Play Center and day camp, "a new plan of out-of-school care was inaugurated." This consisted of full-time summer enrollment for children, with a three-week stay at Northover, plus five weeks of city day camp. The day campers could also use the settlement rooms for informal games, lounges, et cetera. The increased summer programming meant that young and older children would have something fun to do when school was not in session, but it was also a way of expanding what kinds of activities could be offered, both within the rooms Christodora occupied at the Riis Houses and outside the city.

Who Worked There?

The reports distinguished among full-time and part-time workers. Some of those who worked full-time were presumably supervisory personnel and specialists, although it was sometimes hard to tell from the narrative reports how much overlap there was among the different worker categories. On staff for varying periods of time were also volunteers and students doing their fieldwork training or fulfilling other academic requirements. Some of those working at Christodora, both in the city and at Northover, were counselors in training. Over the 1949–1956 period, there were generally four or five supervisory staff members, aided by about the same number of full-time staff, anywhere from six to twenty part-time workers (with additional ones hired for the summer programs). There were also volunteers, whose numbers ranged from sixteen in 1950 to twenty-nine in 1955.

The description of staff for the year 1955–1956 illustrates the difficulty in determining the exact number of people who filled the various positions. It was reported that "the city settlement staff" numbered thirty-five and that this included clerical and maintenance workers. "An additional 17 were engaged for the Summer programs in the city. At Northover the full complement of workers was 47" (Christodora House Collection 1956). In addition to these staff members, there were three people in general administrative positions that year. These numbers indicate that both the city and the camp facilities depended on volunteers and student workers who were supervised by a smaller number of full-time staff and specialists. Interestingly, board

members and former counselors told me in formal and informal interviews that as time went on, more and more of the counselors and supervisory personnel came from the neighborhood
and/or were alumni of the different Christodora programs.
Apparently, this was true both for Christodora as a settlement
house and the Christodora organization that emerged later.
Increasing representation of local community members in the
ranks of volunteers and professionals in these social service
organizations was a significant departure from the original settlement house model, in which most of the workers were people
who came from outside the neighborhood. Once situated in the
neighborhood, however, there were also many settlers and volunteers who stayed for years or relocated permanently to areas
of the city where settlement houses were most common.

NORTHOVER CAMP

The camp outside the city had been central to Christodora operations since the early 1900s and remained so after the move
from Avenue B. Northover Camp was frequently mentioned in
the annual reports as being an intrinsic part of what Christodora House could offer the children and adults of New York City.
A note in the Christodora House records on October 31, 1917,
reported on activity from the past summer: "The Northover
Camp report read by Miss MacColl showed that 550 persons
spent vacations of from three days to six weeks at Northover"
(Christodora House Collection 1917). Informational material
from the early 1930s stated that there was room for 150 campers
of all ages and described the living arrangements: "The younger children have their own quarters, dining room, and activities. The mothers have a quiet retreat for themselves. Bungalows
and tentalows buried in the woods accommodate the older

girls, and the boys have a typical masculine sanctuary with a view that is hard to match" (Christodora House Collection 1930).

Northover became increasingly important to the settlement once the organization became Christodora Inc. in 1952 and after extensive improvements to the facilities had been made. The work that was done in the Bound Brook, New Jersey, location included repairs and expansions of the buildings, making the roads to the camp more accessible, and updating the water and heating systems, all of which helped the organization accommodate greater numbers and types of campers. In addition to the children who attended camp in July and August, the location also hosted a wide range of church, civic, and private groups in the spring and fall seasons, the number of attendees ranging from about twenty to over one hundred individuals at a time. In 1952–1953, the groups that came to Northover included the Japanese-American Christian Association, American Youth Hostels, the Council for Clinical Training, Union Theological Seminary, and Christodora House alumni. Inviting alumni to Northover was a valuable way to maintain the connection that former members had with the organization and camp, and alumni gatherings also encouraged participation in settlement activities and governance at different levels and stages of life.

FINANCING AND AUTONOMY

Raising sufficient funds to cover the facilities, activities, salaries, and other expenses was a constant source of pressure for all settlement houses, not just Christodora House. Settlements also needed to cope with the reality of political and economic factors such as economic depressions and wars, occurrences that were outside their control. Another variable was how much government funding was available to support settlement work and whether there were conditions or stipulations attached to the grants or other types of funds. Those associated with Christodora were constantly responding to these practical conditions and constraints while also keeping in mind the core principles and values that had guided them since 1897. As New York City and the business of delivering social services changed, and while government involvement added layers of bureaucracy to providing needed services and programs, social settlements and other community-based organizations needed either to adapt or close their doors.

From the mid-1800s through the 1920s, financing for settlement houses came mostly from donations and forging relationships with individuals and businesses possessing the capital and expertise to support large projects. In the case of Christodora House and University Settlement, both located on the Lower East Side, donors also provided money for purpose-built settlement house building. This mode of financing prevailed for a number of years:

> In the early years, financing and oversight structure were loose, spontaneous, and personal. Early settlement leaders believed that the very idea of an organized institution contradicted their goals of neighborly reciprocity and informality.... The combination of informal structures and informal financing based on personal relationships enabled settlements to maintain a significant degree of independence. (Fisher and Fabricant 2002, 7)

This "informal financing" was very evident in the Christodora House records. Every year, there were letters from Christina MacColl and other representatives of the settlement house asking for donations or thanking donors. Often this correspondence was tied to specific goals, such as the "Keep a Kiddy at Camp" drive. Particularly poignant were the letters reminding a donor or organization of a financial pledge they had made or announcing an urgent improvement on Avenue B or at Northover Camp. There were also frequent mentions in the board meeting minutes of shortfalls at the end of a year or a projected deficit for the following year. Christodora House was hardly alone in its relentless fund-raising efforts. Even well-known settlement houses had to work hard to make ends meet. Jane Addams of Hull House remarked, "We were often bitterly pressed for money and worried by the prospect of unpaid bills, and we gave up one golden scheme after another because we could not afford it" (Addams 1910, 89).

In 1938, in a case that went all the way to the New York Supreme Court, Christodora House won a legal battle that had jeopardized its future. A previous legal judgment required Christodora House to pay taxes on the upper floors of the sixteen-story building that contained the Club Residence. Ultimately, it was ruled that since Christodora House and the YMCA's William Sloane House were used for educational and charitable purposes, both should be exempt from taxes (*New York Times* 1938). As described in the previous chapter, Christodora faced another financial crisis in the late 1940s, one that did not end well for the settlement and forced them to move from the building at 143 Avenue B. Once at Riis Houses, funds were still tight, despite not having to pay rent for the settlement house space.

Another financial battle that Christodora House ultimately lost had to do with funds from the James Foundation. Arthur Curtiss James and his wife had funded the construction of the sixteen-story building in 1928 and they often made up for deficits in the budget at the end of a fiscal year. On June 4, 1941, Arthur James died, less than a month after his wife. A June 26,

1943, article on the terms of Mr. James's will reported that he left over $25 million to charities, which included Christodora House. The sum of $23 million was placed in a trust, the James Foundation. The money was to be distributed within twenty-five years of his death. In the years after Christodora House moved out of 143 Avenue B, more of the funds were presumably still due the settlement house.

A problem with the James bequest occurred shortly after the move from the building on Avenue B. According to the 1949–1950 Christodora House annual report, the trustees of the James Foundation had notified the board and Christodora's attorneys that funds left to the settlement from Mr. James's will from that point forward would be held back:

> Payments would be discontinued because of doubt in their minds of possible changes in our activities following our removal from the Avenue B building. The result was a decision made by the Trustees to have a survey made of Christodora House and its activities, which survey is currently underway. Cessation of these payments presents a formidable problem, as the planning of our operations, both immediate and future, is jeopardized by lack of operating funds. (Christodora House Collection 1950)

Due to the shortage that year, the settlement house was forced to withdraw over $25,000 from its reserve fund. In July of the following year, Christodora House received twenty thousand dollars from the James Foundation, which, while it was welcomed, "does not represent the portion of the income of the Foundation to which we believe Christodora House is entitled, and efforts are being continued to establish our full rights under the terms of Mr. James' will" (Christodora House Collection 1952). Another $20,000 was released in 1953, a large portion of which was carried over for the following year, and in 1954 an additional $25,000 was distributed to Christodora from the James Foundation.

In the meantime, Christodora House and some of the other charities went to court and an initial judgment was rendered in the foundation's favor. The case then went to appeal, "seeking judicial interpretation of the provisions of the will of Mr. James." In 1954, the New York State Court of Appeals affirmed the lower court's decision, concluding that "the will vests broad discretion in the Trustees of the Foundation," and consequently the trustees decided that no further funds would be distributed to Christodora House and some of the other charities named in Mr. James's will (Christodora House Collection 1954). Which of the other charities were affected was not clear, nor did I find any further mention of the review of Christodora's activities that the James Foundation trustees had said they planned to conduct. There were also no specific details on what the trustees objected to or in what way the work in which Christodora was engaged after the 1949 relocation ran counter to the terms of Mr. James's will.

Some of the money that Christodora House had previously put in reserve from the sale of 143 Avenue B to the city of New York was used to purchase the buildings at 84–86 East First Street in 1959. The First Street buildings then became Christodora's official address. The settlement had already been renting the space and conducting some of its programs there for several years before the sale was finalized. Christodora House also bought a residential building at 151 Avenue B, with plans to eventually renovate it to serve as quarters for offices, classes, clinics, and other settlement activities. This plan never materialized, however, and, after renting the building out as apartments and basically breaking even for several years, that building was sold. The acquisition of these additional holdings suggest that Christodora House was determined to continue operating on the Lower East Side, but not necessarily only within public housing. Even after the purchase of the First Street buildings, Christodora still carried out some of its programs at the Children's Center in the Riis Housing Project at 154 Avenue D and the Youth Center in the same complex at 108 Avenue D. It was also reported that Christodora had an office on West Twelfth Street that was a center for youth employment programs operated in association with youth organizations in Bedford-Stuyvesant and Harlem.[2]

Another blow to Christodora House was dealt when the New York City Housing Authority (NYCHA) communicated to the settlement within the first couple of years after the move that the public housing community served by the settlement was in dire need of counseling and social casework services. However, this presented a problem for the settlement, since the current budget and staffing were earmarked for recreational and educational activities. As negative as this turn of events must have seemed at the time, the NYCHA demands also presented an opportunity for those managing Christodora House to reassess their goals and align these both with the work that was currently being done and with what they wanted it to encompass in future years.

THE 1960s: CHARTING A NEW DIRECTION

Leading up to and during the 1960s, Christodora, as a settlement, was at a crossroads. It is difficult to determine if any one reason was the tipping point, but due to extensive changes in how social services were delivered in New York City and an ever-changing neighborhood, the board members decided that their energies might be better focused on their work and related activities at Northover Camp, a facility that they still owned.

In a fourteen-page memo written by Christodora's director, Stephen Slobadin, on January 2, 1962, he described the current scope of the settlement's work at the Riis Houses and in its facility on First Street. At this point, Christodora's clientele was the largely Puerto Rican population in the area, a result of a huge wave of islanders who had relocated to New York City in the 1950s. Christodora's programs for teenagers and senior citizens at that time were well attended and popular. Regarding the older clients, Slobadin remarked, "The only problem we have here is that they would like us to extend the hours of activity we provide for them. The response to this program has been so good that there is no doubt of its need" (Christodora House Collection 1962, 9).

A significant amount of space in the 1962 report is devoted to the need across the board for Christodora's services, including over the summer, versus the limits of Christodora's budget. Specifically, it referred to a request by Jack Anderson, director of the Lower East Side Neighborhoods Association, for expanded programs for neighborhood youth, especially younger teenagers. Anderson had described serious problems with gangs in the area, particular with a group called "the Dragons," and stated that there was an urgent need to build and develop relationships "not only with younger groups, but also with their parents and other adults in this community" (9).

Near the end of the 1962 report is a section devoted to Northover Camp, in which Slobadin outlined the tremendous need for low-cost or free camp programs. "Of all the community services provided in New York City, camping is one activity that is in short supply. Day camping, in particular, has had a remarkable growth in the city as well as the East Side" (10). He described a wide range of camping programs that Christodora could sponsor in the future, including "day camping at Northover, winter weekend camping, expanded sleep-over camping, family camping, and a senior citizens' camp program"(10–11). Addition of different camping programs, however, "would entail a greater outlay of money on our part. Our neighbors cannot afford to pay much in camp fees. Therefore, in order to serve more of them we would need to reduce the number of children who come to us from outside agencies. This would result in a loss of income" (10).

The final pages of Slobadin's report are under the heading "Proposals for Shifting our Work, if Necessary." The two main options he presented were either changing the scope and nature of Christodora's work within the current neighborhood or moving to another area of the city. Slobadin weighed the advantages and disadvantages of discontinuing the work at the Riis Houses and different possibilities for expanding the work at First Street to a year-round program in addition to expanding Christodora's work at Northover Camp. He also considered the possibility of giving up the First Street building and operating "in a store-front setup in conjunction with a recreation program" (12) in combination with providing the kinds of social service programming that the Housing Authority was asking for. It was unclear whether any of the Riis House facilities would still be needed for that and some of the other scenarios he presented.

Slobadin also outlined a possible Christodora Boys' Club outside the immediate area but "within easy accessibility of our First Street building, either in the West 14th to 23rd Street area or in the Williamsburg-Greenpoint section of Brooklyn "just east of First Street across the Williamsburg Bridge." Slobadin was more inclined to the West Side area option, even though he expressed that "both areas are in greet need of community services with little or no service provided by other agencies" (12). After Slobadin mentioned a few other possibilities in the report, including expanding child-care services, he presented a different option, one that proved to be similar to the direction that Christodora eventually ended up taking: "Should First Street and Riis Houses need to be discontinued and a shift to another neighborhood isn't acceptable to our Board, Christodora House could consider expanding our camping program to service all needy children throughout the city. This means that camping would become our only activity" (13).

Slobadin, a child of immigrants himself, ended the report by emphasizing that the community, the city, and their youth should be the ultimate beneficiaries of any decision that Christodora made about the future of the organization:

> This review is made with the aim of stimulating discussion and thought regarding the work of Christodora House. The ultimate objective, of course, is to assure us that we are carrying out our trust responsibly and in the interest of those who need us most. In so doing we can be sure that we are making the best possible contribution toward improving our community and city. More important, we can feel confident that we may be opening the way in some needy youths' eyes to the possibilities of life in America. (14)

CHRISTODORA HOUSE: THE BUILDING

In 1898, after one year at the Young Women's Settlement at 163 Avenue B, Christodora had moved down the street to 147 Avenue B, where, as Christodora House, it thrived for thirty years. Children and adults streamed in and out of the building all day long and into the evening. The building was extremely spacious

compared with the cramped rooms and cellar of the initial settlement house location. When Christina MacColl had first
stepped into the building at 147 Avenue B, she wondered how
they would ever fill it, but fill it they did.

Then "the Skyscraper"

In 1928, the four-story building at 147 Avenue B (which had been
combined with the one next door some years earlier) was
replaced by a modern sixteen-story building at 143 Avenue B.
With the financing and cooperation of Arthur Curtiss James
and his wife, Harriet, the older structures at 143, 145, and 147
Avenue B and an adjacent house on Ninth Street had been torn
down to make room for the new building. Christodora House
was designed by Henry C. Pelton, also the architect of Riverside
Church in Manhattan.

The work that was done between 1928 and 1948 at Christodora House is described in detail in chapter 4. A complete
account of the structure can be found in Blunt's 2008 article,
which focuses on the building as both a settlement and a residence. The title of the article includes the descriptive words "skyscraper settlement," citing Robert Steel, who claimed that
Christodora House at the time was "the world's tallest structure
dedicated to social service" (Blunt 2008, 550). In her article, Blunt
emphasizes the role of the "club residence" and draws attention
to the ways in which the building's height and size affected both
how it was perceived and used. "Unlike the previous adapted
tenement buildings occupied by Christodora House, and unlike
neighboring tenements around Tompkins Square, the 'skyscraper settlement' was new, large, imposing, and modern: a
'big thing' . . . that changed and dominated the surrounding
urban landscape" (558).

Christodora House as Symbol

When people talk about the structure that is Christodora House, the conversation is often framed in terms of the building's reputation or symbolic significance. In its lifetime, the building at 143 Avenue B has served many purposes and come to symbolize different things to different people. Built in 1928 it was originally a bold experiment—a sixteen-story building that symbolized progress and modernity and aspiration. Since it was built to house a settlement on the first five floors, there was ample space for clinics, classes, and studios as well as facilities for recreation and artistic performances. It also served as a place where workers, the settlers, could live comfortably. The other occupants, known as club residents, occupied the top floors and many of these individuals volunteered to help with the work of the settlement house.

In 1948, the building ceased to house a settlement and the structure was essentially in limbo for several decades. The city of New York took over the building from the settlement, but plans for its use were never fully realized. During the 1960s and 1970s, Christodora House was just one of the casualties of deterioration and neglect in that part of the city. The Puerto Rican activist party the Young Lords set up an office in the building in the late 1960s (Bagchee 2018), and different accounts also place the Black Panthers there for a time (i.e., Mooney 2008). At one point there was hope that the building would be used as a community center, but friction between community members and representatives of the city of New York eventually resulted in an impasse and "in February 1969 police from the Ninth Precinct raided the building and forcibly closed it, enforcing an eviction notice" (Gordon 1994, 222).

Figure 5.1. A man riding a bicycle past the Christodora House. Photo ca. 1976, by Edmund Vincent Gillon, Museum of the City of New York.

Subsequently, the city sold the building in 1975 and it changed hands several times before being sold for development of miniums in 1987. As a result, Christodora House became a symbol of gentrification in the neighborhood and was an object of anger and frustration. This culminated in the events of August 6, 1988, as protests spilled out from Tompkins Square Park. An article published a week later summarized the conflict: "The protest was born of growing tensions in a rapidly changing neighborhood, where residents of widely varying wealth and values have been thrown together. Some wanted the police to curb disorder in the park, while others insisted that using it freely was a political right" (Purdum 1988). That night, police barriers were used by some in the crowd to smash the doors of Christodora House, and the lobby of the building was vandalized. Protesters chanted "Die yuppie scum!" and a banner reading "Gentrification Is Class War" was posted on the building (Abu-Lughod 1994). Today, Christodora House still towers over the neighborhood and prices for the co-op apartments within it are far beyond the reach of what the majority of those who live in the Chinatown/Lower East Side area can afford. Based on data collected from the 2020 census, the median household income for that area was $46,000, while the median property value was $703,000 (Data USA).

For whatever reason, the general public is unaware of the proud history of the settlement house that occupied the structure at 143 Avenue B, even though there is a red medallion on the building that commemorates Harry Hopkins for his work there and his contribution to comprehensive social programs. The marker on Christodora House is one of many "cultural medallions" placed by the Historic Landmarks Preservation Center that call attention to sites throughout the city where notable New Yorkers have lived or worked. The historical marker for Hopkins states that Christodora House was and still is engaged in a "mission to help alleviate the inequities among the underserved." Today, that lofty claim might ring false to the people who recall the events of 1988 or who look at the building today with its expensive condominium apartments. Most people would also be unaware that Christodora House was a symbol of hope and generosity many decades ago or that there is a Christodora organization that is still operating and traces its history back to this East Village location.

6

CHRISTODORA

Continuity and Transformation

THE PEOPLE WHO WORKED in and with the Christodora settlement house in the past were no strangers to change and the need
to adapt. It was a fact of settlement life that events such as fluc-
tuations in the local population, health crises, and abrupt
changes in the national economy came with alarming regularity and had to be dealt with. In addition to the normal turmoil,
Christodora House had experienced some drastic events that
required major adjustments, reaffirmation of essential values,
and an evaluation of its place in the neighborhood and city.
Despite changes in location over the years, Christodora's work
on the Lower East Side went on, and the commitment to help
improve living conditions in the neighborhood, now more
broadly conceived, and to promote individual and community
health and well-being never wavered.

There is a brief report in the Christodora House records that
was written shortly after the relocation in 1948. In addition to
identifying the activities that were being continued at the Riis
Houses, the ones that had been discontinued, and the half dozen
new activities that had gotten under way since the move, the

author of these pages reflected on the core ideas and values of the settlement house:

> Through it all there must run an abiding belief in what has been called "the settlement idea," an appreciation of the need for informality and flexibility in the settlement programs, an understanding of the intimate and personal relationships between settlement workers and so-called clients as compared with the more rigidly set up organizations such as relief agencies, and a willingness to accept the fact that settlements are, among other things, experimental stations, and out of their experimentation and pioneering have come such lasting things as the visiting nurses, school lunches, foster home service, adult education, etc. (Christodora House Collection 1949)

The sentiments written down over seven decades ago resonate with the goals and programs of the current Christodora organization, which operates from an office in midtown. Flexibility and experimentation have been hallmarks of the organization over Christodora's long history. This has been true whether forging a new path meant supporting arts and music programs along with health clinics in the city, pioneering the model of a mixed-use building that housed social services while also operating as a residence, or, most recently, making access to and learning about nature a critical tool in helping individuals to better understand their potential and possibilities and to broaden perspectives on their future. The independence that was typical of settlement houses in their early years was a major factor that helped cultivate "an autonomous, innovative, and flexible community-oriented practice" (Fisher and Fabricant 2002, 7).

In descriptions of Christodora Inc. that appear in print and online today, representatives of the organization proudly acknowledge its long history and steadfast commitment to New York City youth through its programs and partnerships. The current programs focus on facilitating development of leadership and academic skills among New York City's middle and high school students as these individuals explore their relationship with the natural world around them. In classrooms, parks, and other green spaces across New York City as well as at Christodora's camp in the Berkshire Hills and other wilderness sites, the connection with Christodora House's commitment to urban youth and families has remained strong (Christodora Inc. n.d.).

At the time of Christodora House's relocation and in the decades after the move from 143 Avenue B, the staff and board members faced an important decision regarding the future of the organization and its work and the advantages and disadvantages of the options available. Who was most in need of its services and would the settlement be able to maintain a presence both within and outside the city? Operating programs on the Lower East Side, either in a public housing facility or in its own building on First Street, became problematic as the organization grappled with the question of which services and activities were best left to others to take over and which ones were still important to pursue, given Christodora's limited personnel and material resources. Philosophical and ethical dilemmas arose as fundamental differences regarding the purpose and scope of community programs between the New York Housing Authority and Christodora became increasingly evident.

Christodora ultimately decided to take a risk and capitalize on one of its primary strengths—namely, the camping and outdoor educational and recreational activities in New York City and at Northover Camp that had been part of its work since the early 1900s. Camp Iroquois, the camping program at Harriman

State Park that Christodora also operated in the 1960s and into the 1970s, served large numbers of students in four sessions a year, but the scale did not allow for the kind of bonding between the younger people and the counselors that was manageable in smaller groups. While recreation was still a need for urban youth, a plan was developing to provide educational experiences that went deeper than recreation and could help these young people develop confidence and a type of resilience they could draw on for the rest of their lives. The organization was also committed to give its target audience a voice and agency to find their way and their place in the community and the world.

By 1990, Christodora had a clear vision: When students engage with the world of nature, they acquire a better awareness and understanding of self and of leadership. In the process, youth develop new skills and confidence, which lead not only to personal growth but also to new perspectives on life and their roles in the community. Christodora Inc. was originally a private operating foundation, and in the twenty-first century its Manice Education Center in Massachusetts merged into the larger Christodora organization to become a 501(c) (3) public charity of New York State, the funding for which comes from individuals, foundations, and corporations. Board members, several of whom are alumni of Christodora's programs, play a hands-on role, contributing their professional knowledge and skills to the organization.

CONNECTING WITH NATURE

The core purpose of Christodora's activities and nature-based programs is to foster in individual students a stronger awareness of self and of the immense possibilities for learning and growth they can gain through an enhanced understanding of the natural environment. This view resonates with the practices of place-based education, an approach that focuses on exploring and learning about the natural environment along with the cultural and built environments in which one lives. Proponents of place-based education assert that it can help an individual build a sense of self as well as instill responsibility for one's community (Gruenewald and Smith 2008; Sobel 2004). A growing interest in ecology and environment awareness in the 1960s and 1970s led Christodora to develop programs and partnerships at Northover and in New York City that utilized the study of nature as a means by which young people could develop personally and academically. This was then combined with individual activities and a "ladder of opportunity" aimed at helping young people develop and hone their leadership and other critical life skills.

From the Watchung Hills to the Berkshire Hills

In a conversation with Director Judith Rivkin and one of the board members of Christodora, the question of what makes camp and camping experiences so important prompted a range of responses, and the reasons they gave were wide-ranging (private communication September 5, 2022). They said that being outdoors and away from one's normal life is health-giving and that such experiences provide youth with much-needed recreation. In the process, being outdoors and actively participating helps them build on their physical skills. Camp experiences, they elaborated, also promote community building and teamwork, and they deepen a person's relationship and connection with nature. Finally, they made the point that recreational activities like hiking, canoeing, and backpacking help build preteens' and teenagers' self-confidence, and that these encounters with nature inspire an excitement about learning.

The author of the 1948–1949 annual report described at length the unique benefits that extended camping experiences afforded young people:

Camping days obviously hold more opportunities for "controlled excitement" than do city routines. There are the lusty outdoor games, the treasure hunts, the blazing fires (sans police) . . . or the very stillness of the night, with its small and strange noises . . . the tremendous clap of country thunder, the realization of distances as the valley is viewed from a mountain top, the phenomenal light of a single candle in an open field, or "that's gonna be a frog some day?" (Christodora Collection 1949).

As the New York City metropolitan area spread in all directions, the Bound Brook location of Christodora's Camp Northover became less rural and more suburban. At the same time, the Christodora organization made the decision to find a location in a rustic environment that would be the right setting for challenging wilderness experiences for young people. The thinking was that the new locale would be more remote in the way that Northover had been in the early 1900s. After a two-year search, a suitable eighty-three-acre site with a small nineteenth-century farmhouse was purchased in 1980 in the community of North Adams, Massachusetts.

It was ideal for a new wilderness camp as the property was not only situated in the Berkshire Mountains [sic], but also bounded on all sides by the Savoy and Florida State Forests, thus affording easy access to thousands of acres of public wilderness land. . . . The Manice Education Center was established there, and the following summer saw the beginnings of a camping program, still for New York City youth, but now developing with

environmental and conservation education as its primary focus.
(Christodora Inc. 1986)

It is important to point out that the Manice Education Center was not intended to be a replacement for Northover Camp. Rather, Manice was intended as a more wilderness-oriented program for the warmer months and would take the place (though at a different scale and with different program emphases) of Camp Iroquois. Northover had facilities for year-round operation and had been part of Christodora House from the earliest years. The idea for Northover was to rethink the programs in order to creatively involve New York City youth on a year-round basis. For economic reasons, the board ultimately made the decision to sell Northover Camp and focus on developing programs at the Manice Education Center.

At the Manice Education Center today, summer sessions and school-year field trips serve one thousand New York City students per year. The operating season has expanded beyond the original three months and the camp maintains a ratio of one staff member for every five students. Students have the opportunity to swim in a pond, paddle on rivers, hike on trails in the nearby forests and parks, and navigate, as a team, a challenge course on the center's grounds. There is a science building for conducting scientific experiments and presenting student work, and it also provides a place for meetings and other activities. For city kids, Manice may be providing them with their first opportunity to engage in activities that are commonplace on a farm. These include starting and nurturing seeds in the innovative small teaching greenhouse/classroom designed and built for them by late inventor and engineer James Hardigg of nearby Conway, Massachusetts. Students are also occupied with tending, weeding, and harvesting from the large organic garden and taking care of the chickens, including collecting their eggs, on the property.

There are many opportunities for students at Manice, including wilderness immersion and advanced wilderness programs, as well as additional advanced summer ecology programs in the Berkshire area in which students conduct original research on forest ecology systems and can pursue other projects of interest. Each year of a student's participation builds on past summers of learning, encouraging students to challenge themselves in taking on greater responsibility for self. This then extends to responsibility for one's group and community and thus a greater understanding of the nature of true leadership. Ultimately, scholarship opportunities are offered to some students eager to increase their learning and growth with other outdoor and summer science and college science programs.

Focus on the Urban Environment

The connection with Christodora and the urban environment has never been broken, even though the way in which participants view and experience the city has changed. Christodora House worked closely with the public schools in the past and sponsored field trips to parks and other locations within and outside the city. The organization in its current iteration continues to partner with schools in Manhattan to provide similar experiences, but now with an emphasis on urban ecology, geography, water resources, and the New York City environment. It has also extended its reach to the Bronx, Brooklyn, and Queens. The Christodora programs start with sixth and seventh graders in their earth science or biology classes, and these programs become part of the school culture. Seasonal three-day trips to the Manice Center are also offered to students, with camp sessions organized by age.

Ted Elliman, the first director of Manice Education Center and current Christodora board member, looked back at how they first started working in the public schools:

> In the winter of 1980–81, we began meeting with New York City teachers and youth group leaders to urge their help in recruiting outstanding students. One of our first meetings was with the Director of the Academy of Environmental Sciences on East 96th Street. As we talked through our goals and the organization's history, Cole Genn gently interrupted us. "Gentleman, you need not explain any more. I participated in Christodora programs in the 1950s. You are a great organization, and your reputation has preceded you." With that endorsement we were off and running, recruiting students and educator support from the East Harlem Block School, JHS 45, the American Museum of Natural History, Wave Hill, and the Brooklyn Botanic Garden (Christodora Inc. 2006).

In the early 1990s, Christodora partnered with the education department of the American Museum of Natural History to form an on-site Ecology Club that meets after school hours and also year-round. This was later expanded at the students' request to include a separate high school Ecology Club there (both run by exceptional educator Vickie Mayer), as well as weekend investigatory field trips to Black Rock Forest in the Hudson Highlands. During the years of New York City Parks Commissioner Henry Stern's leadership, the Urban Park Rangers were encouraged to partner with Christodora in creating after-school or weekend Ecology Clubs to work in five of the major New York City parks. This inspired some students—Rakeem Taylor, for example—to ultimately find a career in the

New York City Parks Department. A thirty-year Christodora Ecology Club partnership was run with the New York Botanical Garden on weekends for both junior high school and high school students, taught and mentored by past Christodora students, including one educator, Emilie Mittiga, who is a current Christodora board member.

In addition to its work within schools, Christodora also operates what the organization refers to as its "urban programs." These programs "encourage students to get outdoors, explore, and discover how they can play a part in helping to preserve and protect our earth" (christodora.org) These outdoor programs, named by their participants, include, for example, the New Youth Conservationists, a program for eleven- to eighteen-year-old students in the Bronx, in which youth interact with their local green spaces and give back by completing community-service projects such as cleaning up rivers and clearing invasive species of plants. In the ECO Club, for fourteen- to eighteen-year-old students, participants research the ecology of the city while at the same time learning outdoor skills like hiking and birding. Partners for these and other Christodora programs include the Bronx River Alliance, the New York State Environmental Agency, and the Discover Outdoors Organization, among many others.

FINDING THEIR VOICE

One of the distinguishing features of the settlement house was to provide individuals and families in the neighborhood with what they needed. This required awareness among the staff of what was happening locally and then listening to those of all ages and interests. Christodora House embraced this kind of openness and it has lived on in the Christodora organization.

One form this sensitivity takes is listening to young people and knowing when to stand back to let them develop their own voice. Students who are currently in or are candidates for Christodora programs are asked what they want to do and what they would like to know more about. How do they want to proceed? If a student says he observed dead leaves and the trail of moles, he is encouraged to explore those clues and see where they lead. Counselors and other staff meet students where they are and help guide them to where they want to go.

Working with partners like Hello Insight and other youth-development experts has validated Christodora's attention to the mental health and development of the young people the organization works with. These partnerships have also reaffirmed the centrality of social and emotional learning, a construct that has strong empirical support (e.g., Reppy and Larwin 2019). As a testament to the quality of Christodora's work, the organization has been one of the recipients of Hello Insight's HI Impact Award, an honor that is given to partner youth organizations that have demonstrated success in promoting social and emotional learning with their young clients. Christodora is one of only a handful of youth organizations that have won the HI Impact Award multiple times.

In the past, Christodora staff members decided to rethink how their camping programs were organized, and they realized that not all learning is formal. Much of learning, whether social, emotional, or academic, is tentative and a work in progress. Informality and flexibility were hallmarks of Christodora the settlement, and these characteristics have carried on in the organization of today. Another key aspect to Christodora's work is how vital human relationships are and what part communication plays in establishing and maintaining these bonds. In addition to learning how to communicate effectively, young people are assisted in developing soft skills, such as self-awareness and empathy, which, in turn, are connected with defining oneself and one's goals and being able to work well with others.

LEADERSHIP AND LEARNING

The Christodora organization's print and online information as well as personal accounts all report that students return year after year and routinely develop into staff members and role models. This sustained engagement is enhanced by courses like the High School Leadership Training Course, described as "an intensive experience promoting self and community reliance while discovering existing leadership potential" (Christodora Inc.). The course takes place at the Manice Education Center in the Berkshires, where students attend workshops on topics like decision making, group and social skills, and conflict management. Activities in nature, like navigating and orienteering, are also part of the course, as are natural history lessons, environmental debates, and evening discussions.

The leadership courses are part of a larger "ladder of opportunity" that Christodora offers students. They are encouraged not only to learn how to conduct empirical research but also to cultivate those research skills for use in other areas of life. There is an active alumni program, and the Edward S. Elliman Scholars Program for Advanced Studies in the Environment provides support for students "to pursue their studies in specialized science and wilderness programs, with additional scholarship support from program partners" (Christodora Inc.). Some of the students who participated in this program have gone on to attend the National Outdoor Leadership School and have worked on crews that maintain backcountry trails. The study afforded by the scholars' program helps prepare students for college and careers in environmental science, and to attain outdoor and recreational management positions. What students glean from the leadership and other courses at Manice nurtures a lifelong appreciation for nature and a profound awareness of the interconnectedness of life systems.

CONCLUSION

During the COVID-19 crisis, it was business as usual at Christodora, with adjustments made when warranted. The camp reopened in the summer of 2021, in compliance with health regulations. Students and staff took their temperatures, wore masks, practiced social distancing, and operated remotely when it was possible and appropriate. Students stayed healthy and were deployed into the city parks, now used more than ever by the public but severely understaffed. A Christodora contingent formed teams and called themselves "the rapid response rangers." Self-funded, they picked up trash in places like Crotona Park in the Bronx (known for its variety of tree species) and on the trails. Through their resolve and energy these motivated young people succeeded in playing an active role in the healing of New York City.

In September 2022, Christodora held its annual gala at the Central Park Boathouse in New York City, celebrating 125 years of service to New York City. Based on the theme "Onward," the traditional Christodora hymn, the event was part fund-raiser and part acknowledgment of all the teamwork and determination that have gone into the long tradition of the organization, reaching back to the settlement founded by Christina Mac-Coll and Sara Carson on Avenue B. But mostly the night was a celebration of the young people and alumni who make up not only the present enterprise that is Christodora but who also embody its past and future.

An example of a Christodora alumnus for whom the organization was life-changing is Sin Senh, a 2021 Christodora alumni award recipient and now a Christodora board member. An immigrant from China, he grew up in the Bronx in a family on public assistance. Senh is now a registered professional geologist and CEO of Roux Associates on Long Island, a company that, in his words, "cleans up the environment." In his remarks at the 2021 Christodora gala, Senh related how his math teacher in junior high school had introduced him to Christodora—a common trajectory for many of the students who participate in its programs. He told the audience how he went on a three-day trip to the Berkshires in 1986, not really knowing what to expect. The first morning at Manice, he and the others on the trip went into the woods, where they participated in a trust-building activity that involved falling backward, relying on their classmates to catch them. When Senh was leaving the tree stump where the activity took place, he threw a loose Band-Aid away on the stump. He related how the counselor, Chris, on the spot, "gave me a lecture about bio-degradation like you wouldn't believe. At that moment I had to think about what he was saying to me, you know, kind of reading between the lines. When I left that tree stump I figured I knew what I would do with my life; at least I thought I did" (Christodora Inc 2021).

Senh went back to Manice that summer and for several more. He graduated from Brooklyn Technical High School and eventually received a B.A. in Geology and Environment Studies and an M.A. in Hydrogeology from Binghamton University. Starting as an entry-level geologist in 1999, he went on to become president, CEO, and principal hydrogeologist of Roux Associates twenty-one years later, right before the COVID-19 pandemic. "It's come back full circle, right? Without Christodora, I would not have gained the skills to be a geologist, to be an outdoorsman, to be at Roux." He stood before this audience that was celebrating his and other alumni achievements, having succeeded and now being a member of the board himself. He made it clear what his motivation was:

> The most important thing for me was somewhat self-serving: I want to know that I can have an impact on a younger version of me, some kid from the Bronx or Brooklyn, someone somewhere in the city, someone underprivileged, probably minority, who wasn't given a chance. And we have this place, these programs funded by very gracious people who care . . . At the time I didn't understand why and now I get it. Thank you for this award; it means more than you know for me and for my family. (Christodora Inc. 2021)

Senh's experience with Christodora echoes that of many first-generation college students, teachers, business owners, college professors, tradespeople, and thousands of others who have had different degrees of involvement with the organization. Just as important and worthy of mention are individuals (and there are many) who now have their own families and who may still live in New York City. Not all of them may have achieved the same level of material success, but with the skills, self-confidence, and knowledge they received at Christodora, they can now instill in their own children, families, and friends the value of being thoughtful stewards of the land and waterways and the other precious resources of our natural environment.

Christodora, in its present form, carries on the time-honored tradition of service and commitment to the children and families of New York City. In the words of Pamela Manice, president of the Christodora board, one important ingredient is that many of those who participate in the programs complete that circle of caring: "We help students pursue their interests, and their growth is limitless. They were nurtured and they nurture back" (personal communication, October 23, 2022). It is this cyclical nature of community service and support that is so encouraging at a time when human connection is too often overlooked and undervalued.

Perhaps one of the "gifts" of COVID-19, or Hurricane Ian, or the wildfires in California and the Northwest is the realization of the strength that lies in these human connections. Those who are suffering can take solace in knowing that there are people who recognize that they are in pain or feel isolated and that these people, often strangers, will then come forward and do what they can to help. Christina MacColl devoted her life to this calling, as did those around her and all of those who have followed, including the counselors, board members, teachers, and others who are involved in organizations like Christodora. What they have in common are the relationships they have chosen to invest in and the connections they forge. In the final analysis, what they manage to accomplish, whether large or small, heroic or mundane, can be lifesaving.

PART III

THE SETTLEMENT HOUSE
AND THE COMMUNITY

7

THE SETTLEMENT HOUSE

Motivations, Controversy, and Limitations

EVEN THOUGH THEY SHARE some basic characteristics, every settlement house in the United States is unique, and each of the early ones was influenced by its resident workers and the surrounding neighborhood. The settlement as initially formulated was a social institution embedded within a wider society where certain values were promoted over others. In addition, the original settlement houses came into being during a particular period of time and then adjusted to the political and social climate as well as prevailing assumptions and prejudices. In hindsight, what were the people living in and supporting settlement houses in the late 1800s and early 1900s hoping to accomplish, and why?

A number of historians and social commentators have been critical of the settlement house movement, making claims that conversion to Christianity and assimilation into the "American way of life" were the main reasons for their existence. Others have said that settlement house work was frivolous or no more than glorified etiquette lessons. In reality, the motivations of settlement house workers varied tremendously. While some settlement workers looked down on the immigrants with whom they worked and believed that the latter needed to be "uplifted" and remade, similar perspectives are not uncommon today. In other words, the impulse to assimilate and Americanize immigrants and see them as "the other" was not just limited to the past.

Some of the controversial issues that have arisen regarding the settlement house movement as well as some of the movement's shortcomings will be addressed here. I will be mainly focusing on the topics of racial exclusion (which was also touched on in the chapter on settlement houses) and the roles that religion and cultural assimilation played in the settlement houses and the movement more broadly. Inevitably these topics come up when discussing progressive movements and social settlements in the United States; to gloss over them would be at best misleading and at worst dishonest.

Rather than deny that racism extended to the settlement house or that assimilation and religion and religious conversion were absent among the motivations of settlement workers at the time, it is ultimately more useful to acknowledge the movement's shortcomings and then look at the problems that settlement houses confronted and what they were able to accomplish. We can also ask this question: What would life have been like for immigrants in the settlement house neighborhoods if those institutions and the people responsible for them had not existed? Were immigrants and U.S. society ultimately the better for the settlement houses over the decades? Also, in what ways do new immigrants and the disadvantaged in our cities benefit from present-day settlement houses and community centers? Some of these questions will be addressed here and then will be followed up in the next chapter.

Historical context is an important consideration when seeking out the motives of settlement house workers and others who supported the early settlement houses. The world in which people were living and working over one hundred years ago was very different from the one in which we live now. Because of major differences in values and opinions across historical periods, simply imposing current values and assumptions on events in the past should be avoided. Views toward religion, organized or otherwise, and the ways that longtime residents in the United States felt about the influx of immigrants and women coming to the cities from abroad and from the southern part of the country had a great impact on the social institutions of the day. Does that mean that people who held racist or xenophobic views or believed that a woman's place was in the home were justified in their views and actions? Certainly not, but these views were omnipresent in U.S. society, and anyone resisting these perspectives, and there were many who did, needed to swim against a strong, nearly unyielding tide.

RACIAL EXCLUSION AND THE SETTLEMENT HOUSE

After acknowledging how significant the settlement house movement was in North America, Stebner (2006) offered some clarity on the context in which the settlements were established: "Although as embedded with racism and classism as was dominant society itself, settlement house leaders believed that democracy was best served by social interactions and a sense of social interdependence" (1068). Another assessment of the position of the settlement house movement toward the integration of their institutions is the following:

> In its first forty years the settlement movement did not ameliorate, or even directly address, white society's systematic discrimination against black Americans. Though several of the white

founders of the NAACP had settlement connections, institu-
tionally the settlements failed to make any significant contribution to white Americans' consciousness of racism or to
furthering black people's rights and opportunities." (Carson
1990, 195)

This was a missed opportunity for the settlement house movement. Undaunted, Black social reformers like Ida B. Wells and
Victoria Earle Matthews acted on the need for social services
within their own communities and did not wait for the white
settlement house establishment to change. Hounmenou (2012)
explored the origins and impact of the Black settlement movement and its role in the development of oppositional consciousness in Black communities: "Similar to the Black church, the
Black settlement houses not only played a substantial part in the
social lift of underprivileged community members, but they also
provided spaces for the development and maturation of a culture of resistance that helped to transition to the fight for equal
rights" (663). The author's meaning of "social lift" here is that
Black settlement houses lifted underprivileged community
members socially or helped improve the social status of underprivileged community members.[1]

That said, there were white settlement house leaders who did
not accept the color line in U.S. society and its institutions but,
instead, deplored its effects and the injustices committed against
Blacks through widespread racism and exclusionary practices.
Jane Addams and Florence Kelley, for example, were actively
involved in the formation of the National Association of Colored People (NAACP) in 1909, and other settlement leaders let
it be known that all who needed their services, regardless of race,
were welcome. It would take decades for others to do the same.

THE ROLE OF RELIGION IN THE SETTLEMENT HOUSE

In the early years of the settlement house movement, Christianity was the dominant religion in both England and the United States. The precursor of the American settlement house movement, Toynbee Hall, was established by Anglican clergyman Samuel Barnett. Many proponents of the settlement house in the United States preached a version of the Social Gospel from the pulpit, and they promoted the idea that social reform "must be motivated by the 'power of personal sympathy' and the Christian ethic of personal responsibility" (Carson 1990, 13). Settlement workers at the time were aware of how the settlement house's social reform agenda, influenced by the Social Gospel, differed from that of church-related settlements or missions: "Non-sectarianism, or at the very least, non-denominationalism, was for settlement workers one of the key differences between their institutions and the inner-city missions run by various Christian sects" (James 2001, 60).

The terms *sectarian* and *nonsectarian* were used to refer to those social service institutions that were religious and nonreligious, respectively, at least in theory. In reality, "the lines between sectarian and nonsectarian houses—between missions and settlements—were blurred in the late nineteenth and early twentieth century" (Stebner 2006, 1063). *The Handbook of Settlements* listed the existing settlement houses in the United States and attempted to establish criteria that distinguished between settlements and institutional churches and missions, but these were not clear-cut. The authors included "houses having a high degree of the settlement spirit" in the handbook as long as they did not incorporate religious elements or activities that were "carrying the house in question beyond the distinctive limits of the settlement field" (Woods and Kennedy 1911, v). That would assume, of course, that there were "distinctive limits" at that early stage to what exactly a settlement house was and what it was not. As noted previously, Christodora House was one of the settlements listed in the handbook in a special section entitled "New York City Neighborhood Houses Maintaining Religious Instruction." Jane Addams was more explicit about the difference between religiously oriented settlements or missions and mainstream settlement houses. She maintained that "missions exist to convert people to a particular view, while settlements exist to identify the needs of a neighborhood and thereby improve conditions" (Stebner 2006, 1063).

Some present-day historians have made sweeping characterizations of the social settlement in general as well as specific settlement houses. One author identified Christodora House specifically: "As physical and cultural sites of assimilationist ideals, evangelical social settlement houses such as Christodora and the numerous church-sponsored Protestant missions often evoked mixed reactions from neighborhood residents and religious leaders alike" (Yee 2011, 138). Yee's claim that there were mixed reactions to settlement houses is indisputable, and there is much evidence to support this. However, the blanket characterization of Christodora House as "evangelical" and her supposition that Christodora and "church-sponsored Protestant missions" were sites of "assimilationist ideals" are both, in my view, inaccurate, and I will start with the characterization of Christodora and similar settlement houses as being "evangelical" in nature.

First of all, evangelicalism is complex and multifaceted, and it is difficult to find a serviceable definition today. One element that stands out among the different definitions of evangelicalism is the emphasis on conversion. This resonates with the distinction that Jane Addams made between settlements and missions. Each early settlement house was unique, and Christodora House was largely molded by the personality and belief system of Christina MacColl. Far from being naïve, MacColl was aware that religion was a sensitive issue in the neighborhood, especially with her Catholic and Jewish neighbors. In a way, it was fortunate that the settlement house was called Christodora House, a name whose literal meaning signals a connection with Christianity. However, as MacColl herself stated:

> Enough of God's love can make Catholic and Protestant, Jew and Gentile live in harmony, each expressing the religious belief which he daily learns from God. The settlement ever seeks to emphasize the common grounds, never to emphasize differences. The common ground of our religious life is the fatherhood and love of God, helping every boy or girl, man or woman with whom we come in contact, to realize in a practical way in the things of everyday life, God's real presence, tender love and ever-present strength. (MacColl 1903)

These sentiments clearly convey MacColl's rationale for the work to which she and the other Christodora House workers were devoted. However, even though Christina MacColl was committed to the Christian message in her own life, it does not mean that she was set on imposing her faith on others. Considering the widespread views toward religion when settlement houses first began and then spread throughout the country, expressing a belief in a divine being was hardly out of the ordinary. Neither, I would argue, would the mention of God as a motivating force for socially oriented service have been offensive to the many immigrants who flocked to the settlement for the support and encouragement it offered them. Would MacColl have been pleased if a Catholic or Jewish adult converted to Protestantism?

Undoubtedly she would have, and she said as much in some of her letters. I maintain, however, that Christina MacColl was primarily devoted to combating poverty and inequality and improving conditions in her neighborhood and city. She wanted to ensure that "here, personal service and adaptation as well as culture and wealth are utilized and enter at once into the fiber of humanity" (Christodora House Collection 1902).

ASSIMILATION/AMERICANIZATION EFFORTS AND THE SETTLEMENT

Settlement houses and other organizations, such as the YWCA and the Hebrew Immigrant Aid Society, were sites of assimilation in the sense that they were teaching English, providing job training, and helping people from different countries and backgrounds adjust to life in the United States. These were all commonplace activities at settlements and other social service agencies at that time and up to the present. Helping immigrants understand and adjust to life in the United States was only one goal of the settlement house. Other guiding objectives included helping families stay healthy and happy and encouraging young people to have confidence in their own abilities and aspirations. Those who worked at the settlement were also expected to learn from their experiences with the children and adults in the neighborhood who came from a variety of cultures and spoke a number of languages. Vida Scudder, in reference to the Italian immigrants she encountered, commented, "They are well worth knowing" (Carson 1990, 104). This response to other cultures was echoed by Jane Addams: "Great is our loss when a shallow Americanism is accepted by the newly arrived immigrant, and their national traditions and heroes are ruthlessly pushed aside'" (103).

Radical reformer Emma Goldman had her own opinion about the work done in the settlement house. She had a friend named Emma Lee, who worked at the Henry Street Settlement, and Goldman often visited Lee there. While Goldman admired Lillian Wald and other settlement house leaders for their attention to the economic plight of poor people in the cities, Goldman also commented, "Yet their work seemed palliative to me. 'Teaching the poor to eat with a fork is all very well,' I once said to Emma Lee, 'but what good does it do if they have not the food? Let them first become masters of life; they will then know how to eat and how to live'" (Goldman 1931, 160).

Emma Goldman was not alone; other reformers and union organizers were critical of the settlement house and similar organizations because, in their view, these institutions did nothing to combat the issues of class and economic inequality in the United States. The journalist Rose Pastor Stokes, an immigrant herself, was critical of settlement houses and believed that they only contributed to the divide between the social classes. Gertrude Barnum, a woman who had come from an affluent family, was a resident worker at Hull House and head resident for a time at the Henry Booth House, both of which were in Chicago.[2] Barnum then turned her energies to the fight for fair labor practices and became the national organizer for the Women's Trade Union League. She had come to the conclusion that settlements did not go far enough to make a real difference in people's lives:

> I began to feel that while the settlement was undoubtedly doing a great deal to make the lives of working people less grim and hard, the work was not fundamental. It introduced into their lives books and flowers and music, and it gave them a place to meet and see their friends or leave their babies when they went out to work, but it did not raise their wages, or shorten their

hours. It began to dawn on me, therefore, that it would be more practical to turn our energies toward raising wages and shortening hours. (Crocker 1992, 223)

As valid as Barnum's argument appears on the surface, I would argue that it was through her work in the settlement house that she had gained an intimate knowledge of the lives of the families whose cause she later took up as a labor reformer. In addition, many of those who had come to the settlement would not have been able to work at all if not for child care, or their children would have been left alone to fend for themselves while their mothers were at work. In the end, workers and their families also benefited in substantial ways from the services provided by the settlements, and Barnum's impulse to contribute to social change was made possible both her extensive contact with the settlement house as well as through her subsequent role as worker advocate.

VALUES AND ACCOMPLISHMENTS

In the nineteenth and early twentieth centuries there was a wide gap between rich and poor, and many city dwellers, particularly immigrants, often lived in squalid conditions. One principle on which the settlement house idea rested was that the resident workers, the settlers, establish meaningful relationships with those who had not had the same opportunities as they themselves had had, including a higher education. Sweatshop workers and other laborers in the United States were exploited by their employers, and what the workers earned was often not enough to put a roof over their heads or feed their families. Under these circumstances, it was vital that settlement house resident and volunteer workers take the important first step of connecting with their neighbors and affirming their common humanity. Only then could work in the classrooms and clubs and clinics proceed. Making meaningful connections across class lines was not a simple matter, however, especially because it required both sides to trust and respect each other. As Christina MacColl stated over one hundred years ago, "The trust of the people is our greatest joy. They believe in us and know we mean to be true in all things" (MacColl 1908).

It was because of the faith that many immigrants held in the settlement workers that mothers and fathers who had never seen a dentist were confident that their children would be safe in the hands of clinic workers. Young women who befriended the girls in their clubs became confidantes and sometimes even functioned as intermediary between a child and the school or between a teenager and an anxious parent. In a chapter in *House on Henry Street* on working with young people in the neighborhood, Lillian Wald stressed the importance that those in settlements placed on authentic, long-term relationships: "Intimate and long-sustained association, not only with the individual, but with the entire family, gives opportunities that would never open up if the acquaintance were casual or the settlement formally institutional" (Wald 1915, 190).[3]

At the same time, there were also doubts expressed about how genuine the relationships between the workers and their neighbors could be, given the factors that divided them. Robert Woods, founder of the South End House in Boston, privately lamented that "the relation between the settlement and their neighbors is an artificial one. I don't know if it can ever be otherwise" (Carson 1990, 60). One factor that made a difference in the quality of the relationship between neighbor and settlement worker was the length of time a settler remained in the neighborhood and the depth of empathy she was able to cultivate for her neighbors. Christina MacColl was described as "the soul of the neighborhood" due to her many years living and working at Christodora House, and many residents, particularly females, lived in the settlement house for extended periods of time. Their long-term investment in the house and the neighborhood proved to be consequential and was a powerful antidote to the kind of artificiality to which Woods was referring.

CONCLUSION

In a study of three settlement houses in Indiana, including two Black settlement houses, the author summed up their everyday activities: "Thousands of people, young and old, black and white, Americans and immigrants, came to settlement classes, clubs, and socials, used settlement facilities, and attended settlement events" (Crocker 1992, 224). In answering the question of why they came, Crocker concluded, "People came to the settlement because they needed what it had to offer." Settlement houses across the country provided clean, safe spaces in which immigrants and other city dwellers could meet with their peers and with settlers, whom they often viewed as teachers. The settlement was also a pathway for many to a better education, citizenship, and higher-paying jobs. The settlement house movement, even with its flaws, "provided an amazing response to social problems and questions regarding individual and community development. . . . Immensely successful in addressing a host of issues, the movement also provided (mainly but not exclusively) white middle-class women with significant personal ties and professional opportunities" (Stebner 2006, 1068). Many of these women, Black and white, became the social workers and social reformers who went on to apply what they had learned in the settlements to establish other social service organizations, pass important legislation, and work in government agencies that, with time, would contribute to social change.

8

THE SETTLEMENT HOUSE

Impact and Adaptation

THE SETTLEMENT HOUSE IN the late 1880s and early 1900s came into being because there were men and women, clergy and lay-people, professionals and students, who recognized the need for an immediate response to the overcrowded cities and lack of social services for the poor. In contrast to Gertrude Barnum's claim that the settlement house did not adequately address economic issues among the poor, settlement house workers were at the forefront of reforming child labor laws and shortening the workweek. On a grassroots level, there were many leaders and other workers in the settlement house movement who actively supported labor unions and striking workers, sometimes at their own peril. In the University Settlement's 1901 annual report, it was noted that "[We] are probably the only social settlement in the city, or for that matter, in the whole country which has so extensively put in practice the policy of becoming a labor center. Eleven unions meet at the settlement for regular sessions" (Weissman and Heifetz 1968, 43). There was also an anecdote in the Christodora House record about newsboys coming together in the settlement to discuss an impending strike. Although some settlement houses did not encourage discussion of current topics that were politically charged, places like University Settlement and Christodora House provided a safe haven for workers who were coming into conflict with their employers or with industries such as the needle trades and meatpacking.

RESEARCH AND THE SETTLEMENT HOUSE

One of the ways in which the settlement impacted their communities was by collecting data on everyday social problems such as income inequality and inadequate sanitation and housing conditions. One of the three Rs of settlement work was research, and the empirical studies in which the settlement workers were engaged often led to concrete action either during or beyond the time when the workers lived in the settlement. Some of those who resided in or were otherwise involved in the settlement house have been referred to as "settlement sociologists" (Lengermann and Niebrugge-Brantley 2002, 9). These individuals and groups conducted systematic studies that examined the living and working conditions of the urban poor. Many of these investigations yielded statistics and profiles that were difficult for authorities and employers to dispute. The work of the settlement houses and the care with which they conducted their research evolved into contributions to the health and welfare of workers and families that were far more comprehensive than any research that had been done previously. "The settlement workers' involvement with public health reform grew out of their inductive approach to social work, and their focus on the neighborhood as the primary social unit" (Carson 1990, 72).

One example of how this inductive approach was translated into concrete action was when the residents of South End House in Boston conducted detailed studies of conditions that were in need of reform in their city. *The Handbook of Settlements* described the area surrounding South End House as "a mixed factory and tenement quarter in an increasingly congested section, with much old housing, and generally adverse conditions" (Woods and Kennedy 1911, 128). The residents of South End House surveyed housing in the South End and other parts of Boston, determined to improve conditions and hold local government accountable to laws that were already on the books. The results of this study contributed to official enforcement of the building code.

A more extensive and multifaceted research project was conducted by Florence Kelley, a social and political reformer who was a resident of Hull House between 1892 and 1894. Kelley and several other settlement residents embarked on a detailed study of Chicago's Nineteenth Ward as part of a national study Congress had commissioned on the slums of selected American cities.[1] Kelley and her team, some of whom had been dispatched from the U.S. Department of Labor, painstakingly gathered information on the nationalities and wages of local residents. They knocked on doors and visited the homes and workplaces of the local residents, including the dozens of sweatshops in the neighborhood. The result was the volume *Hull-House Maps and Papers,* published in 1895. Subtitled *A Presentation of Nationalities and Wages in a Congested District of Chicago,* the book features essays that thoroughly document the economic and social conditions endured by immigrants in that working-class neighborhood. The entire undertaking was both courageous and groundbreaking: "It is one of the first publications that refuted conservative laissez-faire economics with statistical data on wage labor. It is one of the first publications that graphically details the plight of immigrants and documents their work ethic, blaming the economic system rather than the individual for social conditions in the slums" (Residents of Hull-House 2007 [1895], 3).

Even though social research studies like those in Chicago and Boston were initiated and carried out by the residents of the local settlement houses, the work relied on the trust and cooperation of the neighbors to answer questions and provide information about themselves and their families. While we will never know how truthful the research participants were in every instance, local residents became valuable partners in the documentation of conditions in their neighborhoods. The results were widely disseminated, and the entire research study opened the public's eyes to how immigrants lived and how they were contributing to the U.S. economy and prosperity, which others were able to enjoy.

SETTLEMENT HOUSE SERVICES AND PROGRAMS: THEN AND NOW

Settlement houses have always had an open-door policy. Neighbors are welcomed and listened to in the current settlement and community houses, and initiatives like public baths, improvement of and expanded access to housing, and low-cost or free child care were direct results of needs expressed by those who lived in the tenement neighborhoods. The ability to adjust to current circumstances was one of the hallmarks of the original settlement house movement, and it was reflected in the attitude of the workers toward their mission and clientele. "Settlement houses were born in a spirit of improvisation and flexibility, motivated by the idea that they would provide services, as needs arose, to the neighborhoods in which they were located" (Batlan 2005, 236).

The settlement house filled a genuine need at a point in history, after which time some of the houses and organizations evolved, while others eventually ceased to exist.[2] Immigrants moved out of many of the neighborhoods in which settlement houses were located, or other agencies took over some of the responsibilities and services. Professional social workers now made home visits, followed up on reports of families who needed financial and other kinds of assistance, and the public schools had counselors and other personnel who could identify when children and their families had need of particular programs or services. That is not to say that these developments were always adequate to the task, but at least some of the work of the settlement was delegated to different organizations, social workers, and health professionals.

Today, a settlement house is defined as "a neighborhood-based social organization that provides services designed to identify and reinforce the strengths of individuals, families, and communities. Settlement house programs build bonds, create networks, promote advocacy, and develop connections both within organizations and throughout the wider community" (United Neighborhood Houses). This is in many ways what settlement houses have always done, but the emphasis now is more on strengths, as opposed to the deficit-oriented approach of a century ago. Henry Street Settlement describes its current community in terms that emphasize how those in the area contribute to the character of the neighborhood and city: "The rich cultural, racial, and ethnic diversity of our community underlies a sense of community among residents, providing a strong foundation for our Community Board; a vibrant artistic community; and culture-based values among many families that emphasize the involvement of the extended family in the care of children as well as older adults" (Henry Street Settlement).

The settlement houses in New York City that still exist, whether as a settlement, community center, or other form of nonprofit organization, have all set their own course since being established in the late nineteenth century. For example, ever since 1886, the University Settlement Society, the oldest settlement house in the United States, has "collaborated with our communities to pioneer highly effective programs that fight poverty and systemic inequality" (University Settlement Society). The University Settlement has operated since 1898 from the six-story structure on Eldridge Street, built as a settlement house, and its longevity, according to Director Melissa Aase, has been largely due to embracing the valuable qualities of "being a risk taker, evolving, being willing to change, not afraid to embrace mergers and acquisitions, build housing, cross different areas of work" (personal communication, August 22, 2022).

Some of the most common programs and services that were found at the settlement in the past and are still available in settlement and community houses include the following:

- Job training and employment programs
- Child care
- Recreational facilities, classes, and programs
- After-school youth programs
- Classes for adults and children
- English for Speakers for Other Languages (ESOL) and literacy education
- Citizenship instruction and guidance/advice with government regulations and requirements

In addition to many of the services that settlement houses have always provided, the settlement house of today often provides home care, housing, and senior centers, home-delivered meals, and mental health services. Even though psychological services and care have long been needed in urban communities, it took many decades for mental health services to be considered as vital to a community's well-being as other types of medical care. Because settlement houses have historically been grounded in their communities and mindful of the population's needs, they have been and continue to be well suited for responding to the mental health needs of those in the neighborhood. Hamilton-Madison House, founded in 1898 and located on New York City's Lower East Side in the Two Bridges/Chinatown area, provides behavioral health services for local residents, particularly the large Asian community. These include "outpatient services that strive to maintain the mental well-being of community residents through culturally appropriate prevention and treatment of emotional and/or social difficulties" (Hamilton-Madison House). This complements its Immigrant and Community Services, where newcomers can receive a wide range of legal and financial assistance as well as translation services. They can also get help completing applications and other forms. The mental health and immigrant services combination is important for those who are new to the city and the country, especially since many of them experience racial or ethnic discrimination and harassment along with the normal stressors of being an immigrant living in an urban environment.

Finally, settlement houses have long been known for their quick response to needs that arise suddenly and that only compound issues already prevalent in their communities. Similar to how teenagers who worked with Christodora in the Bronx responded to the overuse and understaffing in public parks during COVID-19, young people on the Lower East Side formed the Henry Street Settlement Community COVID Response Team, which then evolved into the Community Response Team (CRT). The CRT started as a group of twenty young adults, ages eighteen to twenty-four, who were hired to tackle the issue of food insecurity and other critical needs of the community. They "set up personal protective equipment distribution sites in public housing developments, providing residents with masks, gloves, and hand sanitizer; they registered prospective voters. Additionally, the team coached seniors on using the internet to stay connected with loved ones during the lockdown" (Smith 2022). This continues the tradition of the settlers who once lived at Henry Street and other settlements throughout New York City. The fact that these young people incorporated voter registration and technology assistance is an excellent example of how those connected with settlement houses and the organizations that succeeded them rise to the occasion and put their own skills and know-how to use, with the goal of serving and improving their communities.

9

COMMUNITY BUILDING AND ADVOCACY IN THE EAST VILLAGE/LOWER EAST SIDE

THE NEIGHBORHOOD IN WHICH Christodora House is located is a main character in the story of the settlement house and the years that followed. Called "the East Side" by locals a century ago, the part of the historical Lower East Side where Christodora House still stands was home to immigrants from all over the world who came in massive numbers to work and live in New York City. Immigrants continue to be drawn to the area and now, as in the nineteenth and early twentieth centuries, the area is bustling with children, families, and merchants who occupy the four- and five-story tenement buildings. Tompkins Square Park is a place where children play and where adults gather and take a break from city life. Since the 1800s, the park has also been a site of protest and political activity for groups like striking workers and AIDS crisis activists.

One of the purposes of writing about the area surrounding Christodora House is to convey a sense of the ever-changing nature of a neighborhood of creative, resilient individuals and groups of people. That was true in the past and remains so to this day. Many of the neighborhood residents have come and gone through the years, but there is a core faction that still stands firm and is fiercely protective of the "Good Old Lower East Side." What is now called the East Village, Alphabet City, Loisaida, or even still the Lower East Side has seen periods of hardship along with more encouraging times. From the time of peak immigration to the present day, settlement houses, cultural centers, and faith-based, neighborhood, and social service organizations have provided assistance to those in need. This has taken many forms, including food, counseling, medical care, legal assistance, or just a shoulder to lean on. Musicians, painters, writers, and photographers of different races and ethnicities have long found a home in this part of New York City. These include Allen Ginsberg, Miguel Piñero, Jean-Michel Basquiat, and Nan Goldin.

A number of longtime residents have remained active in the East Village and other parts of the Lower East Side, an area that has been built and rebuilt over the decades. These residents have been joined by relative newcomers who call the neighborhood home and who are determined to help it retain the best aspects of its character. Even to call it a single community is inadequate. The East Village has always contained communities within communities in the geographic area they share, but when a crisis or a common cause has arisen, such as zoning changes in the neighborhood or the COVID-19 pandemic, the myriad groups have been known to show a solid front and come together. Community building consists of the motivations and, above all, the work that people put in to make a part of the world, however large or small, a better place.

Like other parts of New York City over the decades, the East Village has had its share of unrest, homelessness, and poverty. Gentrification and changes in the economy have also taken their toll. Areas in the city that have managed to retain some of their historical features and where working-class people can afford to live are shrinking and disappearing at an alarming rate. "The character of the Lower East Side (LES) is changing much faster than its longtime residents would like. Neighborhoods like Chinatown and the East Village, which once housed immigrant communities and avant-garde artists, have gradually ceded territory to small galleries and luxury apartment buildings" (Small 2018). Affordable housing and survival of local businesses are issues on the front lines of the struggle. In addition, income disparities in different sectors of community districts have consequences for funding of community-based services and organizations that rely on various forms of government support. Despite forces that threaten to wipe out the distinctiveness of this part of the city, resourceful residents have continued to put their stamp on it and contribute to its unique atmosphere.

TOMPKINS SQUARE PARK

Tompkins Square Park, a ten-and-a-half-acre public park, is a central feature in the area where Christodora House was constructed and still stands. Created in 1834, the park forms a square bounded by East Tenth Street to the north, Avenue B on the east, East Seventh Street on the south, and Avenue A on the west. The park was originally intended to be a market square, but it has served the public in ways that the planners could scarcely have imagined. It has been renovated and refigured several times and is a place where children can run around, chess players can match their skills against one another, and teenagers and adults can burn up their energy on the basketball and handball courts. For many, it is simply a refuge from the surrounding city and a place to rest or chat in the shade of the park's trees. Groups have gathered in the park for a range of purposes, including outdoor concerts, protests, and, for some who had nowhere else to go, it has served as a makeshift home, especially in the years when there was a permanent band shell.[1] In a history of Tompkins Square Park, the authors attribute its lasting popularity and mixed reputation to several factors:

> Throughout its history, the park was recognized by locals, reformers, and city planners as an important neighborhood resource.... The style of landscape design, the kinds of recreational facilities to be provided, and the range of social organizations encouraged or permitted within its space have all been seen as critical influences on the character and beliefs of generations of users. Perhaps for these reasons, Tompkins Square has achieved a fairly high degree of visibility within the city, despite its size and working-class character. (Reaven and Houck 1994, 82)

Tompkins Square Park has played a key role throughout New York City history not only as a place of recreation and leisure but also as a site of protests and struggle over who belongs there and who, according to some people and the city government, does not. Disturbances in the park, variously called "protests" or "riots" or "altercations," have happened with some regularity since the 1800s. In 1988, there was the Tompkins Square Park riot, during which Christodora became a target due to some associating the building, now condominiums, with the ongoing gentrification in the neighborhood.

THE NEIGHBORHOOD

There have been many characterizations of the neighborhood around Christodora House and the nearby streets. I would use the word *scrappy* to describe the East Village today, both because of its outward appearance and its character—determined and ready for a fight if the need should arise. In my view, the history of the neighborhood and what it is like today support that depiction. There are some excellent accounts of the history of the Lower East Side and the East Village by authors who have depicted and analyzed the various and sundry social movements over the decades that are illustrative of this part of New York City. These include Maffi's book on ethnic cultures on the Lower East Side, Abu-Lughod's comprehensive and insightful study entitled *From Urban Village to East Village,* and Mele's work chronicling "culture, real estate, and resistance" on the Lower East Side. Also important from both a grassroots and macro perspective is Bagchee's *Counter Institution,* a book that contemplates the interactions among architecture, the urban environment, and political systems on the Lower East Side. This is only a partial list of publications about that part of the city. I cannot hope, nor do I try, to provide as comprehensive an account here of the history and social activism of the East Village.

I have chosen instead to highlight a few organizations that provide support to the residents of the East Village/Lower East Side today and the ways in which such organizations help preserve the unique character and creative vibe of the larger community. Featured are groups whose workers, directors, volunteers, and others uphold a culture of resistance, resilience, and sustainability. They do this through their values but especially by their actions. *Sustainability,* in its core meaning, refers to the ability to keep something at a certain rate or level. This encompasses the idea of conserving and/or renewing resources on different levels: environmental, economic, and social. The organizations featured here also advocate for diversity and social justice on behalf of those who live in this area. In particular, community organizations and service providers support those who wish to remain in the

East Village and nearby neighborhoods in the face of odds that are decidedly against them.

Crucial to the enterprise of safeguarding the East Village and surrounding areas of Manhattan are people, factions, and organizations involved in community activism and historic preservation. There are also those who fight for the rights of girls, the poor, and the LGBTQ community. The banner of the Puerto Rican residents and artists who first coined the place name Loisaida is still carried proudly, and other individuals and groups stand for the homeless and disenfranchised who live in the East Village and on nearby blocks. Rent strikes, protests, free meals, and provision of health and mental services are not just relics of the past, and some of the original settlement houses, such as Henry Street Settlement and University Settlement, are actively providing programs and services to bridge the gap between what local residents need and what is readily available to them. Newer community centers and social service agencies have also stepped in, and those who run the local arts organizations and community gardens have done their part to keep the creative and resource-conscious spirit of the East Village and other parts of the Lower East Side alive.

ORGANIZATIONS AND ADVOCACY

Specific topics that have been central to the East Village community as a whole and have served as rallying points for organizations and neighborhood residents are housing, local businesses, youth services, and culture and the arts. These broad themes have long been important considerations in New York neighborhoods, although residents in different eras have not always dealt with them in the same ways, depending on what was happening outside their borders and which factors were beyond their control. After all is said and done, I fully agree with the statement "Neighborhood initiative, like the communities it serves, remains strangely powerful, even in its vulnerability" (Halpern 1995, 232).

Housing

One of the distinctive features of the Lower East Side are the tenement buildings that are typically four to six stories tall. The dictionary defines *tenement* in neutral terms as simply a group of rooms in a larger unit or building, but the word has come to have a number of connotations, mostly negative, in the context of New York City. "Tenement homes are part of the city's history, architectural look, and sociology, as well as the lifestyles of its current residents. The imprint and influence of the New York tenement are layered upon the city much like the apartments themselves are layered atop each other" (Nigro 2018). Zoning laws and housing regulations that have been passed over the years have limited the building of tall structures in residential areas like the Lower East Side. In fact, there are structures on the Lower East Side and other parts of New York City that would not be allowed to be built today.[2]

As a result of deteriorating conditions in tenements in the 1800s and early 1900s, a series of laws were passed to regulate their design, prescribe minimum sanitation facilities, and prevent abuses by landlords who were more interested in making a profit than in understanding how people lived from day to day. These laws were effective only to a certain point; for example, provision of fire escapes was part of the Tenement House Act of 1867, but it was not always followed, or at least not to the letter (Plunz 2016). For immigrants, one of the signs of success was to move out of the tenement neighborhood, and thus there was little motivation for property owners to improve city buildings or blocks. "Despite cultural and political changes, the exploitative housing economy of the slum functioned profitably, providing minimal shelter to wave after wave of impoverished newcomers and making changes . . . only when forced to do so by the state or the collective action of residents" (Mele 2000, 76).

In 2022, after the worst wave (to date) of the COVID-19 pandemic, renters who had received discounted rates in the early part of the pandemic were priced out of their apartments. (Bocanegra 2022). The median property value as reported in the 2020 census in this part of Manhattan was over $700,000, while the median household income was only $46,000 (Data USA).[3] Assistance with finding and holding on to housing, a perennial issue in New York and other large cities, is especially important when regulations regarding rent and leases change or when shifts in the economy or job market occur.

Good Old Lower East Side (GOLES)

One of the main areas of advocacy in which a number of the nonprofit organizations in the East Village and other parts of the Lower East Side engage has to do with housing and tenant rights. One example is GOLES, which works toward "keeping people in their homes and community." (GOLES). Founded in 1977, the organization describes itself as "a grassroots organization that serves, engages, and empowers low- and moderate-income residents of the LES/Loisaida, specifically people of color, through direct services, public education, and community organizing." (GOLES). GOLES provides local residents with information and counseling on their rights as tenants and help in communicating with and responding to landlords. The organization also helps tenants navigate the minefield of regulations associated with living in public and other forms of housing.

Good Old Lower East Side also cofounded LES Ready!, a long-term recovery group that engages in advocacy, resiliency planning, disaster response, and community drills, and it is designated as a Community Organization Active in Disaster (COAD). Along with GOLES, LES Ready! distributed food and water to keep people alive, let alone in their homes, and played a vital role after Hurricane Sandy and during the pandemic. Tenants in NYCHA housing in particular are especially vulnerable when electricity or essential services are disrupted.

Settlement Houses

In the past, settlement houses in Lower Manhattan were active in helping individual tenants find housing and negotiate with landlords, and settlement house leaders were on the front lines of local, state, and national housing legislation. Henry Street Settlement and University Settlement, both located and still active on the Lower East Side, continue to carry out housing-related work, and this has only become more necessary in recent years. University Settlement, located on Eldridge Street, is committed to providing information and services that build on what has always been an important issue on the Lower East Side:

> University Settlement's Project Home combats homelessness by advocating for safe and affordable housing for all New Yorkers, and by partnering with tenants who are at risk of losing their homes to prevent evictions—including by addressing leasing issues, pushing back against landlord harassment, advising people going through housing court proceedings, and supporting tenant organizing. (University Settlement House Society)

Local Businesses

Over the decades, protestors and activists have resisted property developers' efforts, in particular those funded by outside investors who have used scare tactics and other questionable techniques to gain control of individual buildings and areas in the neighborhoods that make up the historical Lower East Side, including Chinatown and the East Village. Time after time, the developers have prevailed or used legal loopholes to their advantage. Lin (1994) refers to the result as an "invading gentrification frontier," a phenomenon that has led to "displacing not only residents but the existing configuration of 'mom and pop' shop and property owners" (58).

When rents rise in neighborhoods or property values rise substantially, small business owners who rent are often forced to relocate. Some shop owners and nonprofit agencies who also own the property where they conduct their business end up moving to other parts of New York City or leaving the city altogether because it makes the most sense for them financially. This makes room for "formula retail" establishments to take their place, and with time neighborhoods are left with only chain stores.

East Village Community Coalition

My initial contact with nonprofit organizations in the East Village was Laura Sewell, executive director of the EVCC. Her office is on the ground floor of Christodora House, on Avenue B, and I interviewed Laura about her organization's work and role in the neighborhood. She directed me to EVCC's website, which features a section on retail diversity and the "Get Local!" directory and "What's Open" map, showing which local businesses, "the lifeblood of the East Village," are operating, along with their hours of operation. This was especially crucial in 2020 and 2021, when New York City was an early epicenter of the pandemic. Laura was one of the authors of the 2022 storefront trends report described below, and her organization is active in sponsoring community events and promoting the preservation of the historically significant built environment of the East Village. The EVCC also supports a number of sustainability initiatives in the area.

Cooper Square Committee

Cooper Square Committee is another local nonprofit organization that is involved with small business development in the area. It also engages in important work toward making housing affordable and supports both residential and commercial tenants. The organization describes itself as "the oldest anti-displacement organization in the U.S.," and its members are proud of their role as "tenacious organizers who have been fighting for 60 years to preserve this community as the racially, economically, and culturally integrated community that it is" (Cooper Square Committee). This organization, partnering with the East Village Independent Merchants Association (EVIMA), has received grants from the New York City Department of Small Business Services to promote and sustain businesses in the East Village commercial district. The grants have enabled them to hire a full-time project manager and expand and diversify EVIMA's member base.

Joining Forces

A survey conducted by the Cooper Square Committee, the East Village Community Coalition (EVCC), and Village

Preservation surveyed trends in storefronts in the East Village from 2019 to 2021 and found that "the number of vacant store-fronts in the neighborhood grew as many merchants struggled to keep their businesses afloat and some were forced to shutter their doors" (Ellman et al. 2022, 18). Of the over seventeen hundred survey participants with businesses in ground-floor commercial spaces in the neighborhood, 14 percent of them were vacant, which represented a five-point increase since 2019. "Respondents to the Merchant Survey reported that the top three challenges they face relate to their commercial rent/lease, finding skilled workers, and marketing/advertising costs" (18). One of the outcomes of the report is an increased effort to work with "tiny landlords" (owners of one building) who have available storefront space and make connections between these landlords and entrepreneurs who could make use of that space "with a particular emphasis on business categories with low barriers to entry, such as retail and other non-food uses" (19).

Youth Services

Contributing to the well-being of children, from infancy through adolescence, has been one of the greatest achievements of settlements in the United States. Children, unlike adults, were often the first to flock to the local settlement house, often to the surprise of the resident workers. "Contrary to their initial hopes and expectations, the residents found that their clubs, classes, kindergartens, clinics, and summer camps formed a backbone of continuity that ensured settlement survival, not just from year to year, but over decades" (Carson 1990, 52). Among the things the present-day Henry Street Settlement offers the neighborhood is a wide range of youth services, including academic and health support, recreation and sports programs, career development services, and a youth urban theater (Henry Street Settlement). Organizations and services tailored specifically to the young have always been in demand on the Lower East Side, either in the form of a range of programs for a varied clientele or those geared toward a more specific purpose or population. Featured here are two of the latter, one of which is specifically for girls and the other one, which offers Alternative to Incarceration services for youth.

The Lower Eastside Girls Club

In operation since 1996, the Lower Eastside Girls Club (LESGC) serves more than five hundred teenage girls and their families every week, opening up for them "an innovative and comprehensive mix of academic, athletic, entrepreneurial, financial, artistic, cultural, family life and wellness, science and technology, service learning, leadership, and world of work experiences" (Lower Eastside Girls Club). The club is housed in a 35,000-square-foot facility on Avenue D that contains studios and labs for fashion and material arts design, music, film, and photography production, as well as coding and robotics. Their entrepreneurial training program, La Tiendita, provides preparation and employment not only for high school girls but also for mothers on the Lower East Side. The club has had a booth at the Essex Market for over ten years, where they sell girl-made and fair-trade products.

The range of emphases and services available to girls at the LESGC exposes them to the study of and potential careers in STEM (science, technology, engineering, and math) and business, in addition to those in the arts and other fields. In the fifty years since Title IX was enacted (the law that prohibits sex-based discrimination at educational institutions that receive federal funding), women have made some gains in STEM. However, according to a report published in 2018, "men still dominate, making up half of all U.S. employees but 73 percent of the STEM workforce" and "women in science earned about $15,000 less than their male colleagues" (McDermott-Murphy 2022). The author maintains that "culture remains an obstacle" to women studying and working in STEM fields. The Lower Eastside Girls Club is helping to break barriers by providing young women with a safe haven, where they receive mentoring, attend after-school and year-round programs, and receive hands-on experience in STEM, design, graphic arts, and other fields and industries.

Avenues for Justice

On May 21, 2022, the Manhattan district attorney and a handful of New York elected officials unveiled a sign on Avenue B that designated the block between Sixth and Seventh Streets "Avenues for Justice Way." The sign refers to the nonprofit organization that operates what was one of the first Alternative to Incarceration programs in the United States. Founded in 1979, Avenues for Justice (AFJ) was first known as the Andrew Glover Youth Program, named for a police officer and youth justice advocate. In an article on the May 21 event, the author refers to Executive Director Angel Rodriguez and the important work done by the organization: "For more than 40 years Rodriguez and AFJ have diverted countless young people away from jail and into programs so that, instead of sitting in a prison cell, they get a second chance at a productive life in society" (Siegel 2022).

An important aspect of AFJ's efforts is the combination of court advocacy and its office inside the Manhattan Criminal Courthouse. The program offers comprehensive support to young people from the ages of thirteen to twenty-four to help them avoid future crime and focus on living successful lives. In order to achieve both objectives, AFJ provides workforce training, education, and mentoring to young people who are presently involved with the court system as well as to those who have been incarcerated previously. In line with its emphasis on prevention, the organization also identifies and works with young people who are at risk of engaging in crime. It measures its success with data and stories of participants who have beaten the odds. For example, in 2022: "Only 5% of our participants are reconvicted of a new crime within three years of enrolling in our program. In contrast, up to 75% of parolees return to crime three years post release" (Avenues for Justice).

Culture and the Arts

The East Village has long been a magnet for artists of all kinds. In an article on the East Village art scene, one of the interviewees sums up some of the cultural movements that made their way to that part of the city: "In the 1960s, the East Village began to house the counterculture. Beatniks and jazz musicians lived there. There's a seamless line between beats and hippies, while punk was a later manifestation of it" (Rosen 2019). The art scene from the 1960s through the 1980s was in many ways a rebellion against the political establishment as well as the art world as Greenwich Village and SoHo became more gentrified and existing galleries were neither hospitable toward nor affordable for new, cutting-edge artists. According to a second interviewee in the article, in the 1970s there were "[t]alented, visionary people in their 20s who were showing artists in storefront galleries. . . . This was thoroughly alien to the concept of 57th Street and Soho [*sic*] galleries, where everything was codified."

As the years went on, the combined forces of the art galleries and gentrification, in some people's view, was just one harbinger of the end of an East Village art movement. Other artists and critics maintained that the art scene there was too eclectic to ever be called one movement. In the end, "[d]espite the brevity of the East Village art scene, an account of its rise and fall is an important means to understanding the relationship between subculture and urban development and the role of the artist and media in the promotion of place" (Mele 2000, 228).

Fourth Arts Block

Notwithstanding past controversies, art and artists have continued to create and flourish on the Lower East Side. One arts group that is active in the area is Fourth Arts Block, otherwise known as FABnyc. FABnyc describes itself as "a team of artists and organizers working to preserve, sustain, and grow the cultural vibrancy of the Lower East Side neighborhood" (FABnyc). A guide to New York City's arts organizations describes FABnyc as an arts coalition in the East 4th Street Cultural District that is "home to more than a dozen arts groups, ten cultural facilities and seventeen performances and rehearsal venues [and] . . . attracts an annual audience of 250,000, serves 1,500 artists and provides more square feet of active cultural use than any other block in New York" (NYC-Arts).

Founded in 2001 by a partnership among cultural and community nonprofits on East Fourth Street, FABnyc is committed to "sustaining the cultural character and diversity of the community," one that extends from Fourteenth Street to Canal Street and from the Bowery to the East River. Proud of its ethnic and racial diversity and in partnership with the local community, the organization brings artists and art to the neighborhood through collaboration, support of the resilience and vitality of the community, and a commitment to increase equity and access to the cultural resources of the Lower East Side and its public spaces. It is also involved in the fight against "physical and cultural displacement," a goal shared by many of the organizations described in this chapter (FABnyc).

The umbrella organization that is FABnyc participates in the Lower East Side History Month and the annual Open House weekend in the neighborhood. It has also sponsored Load OUT!, a reuse and recycle event aimed at transforming one person's trash into another person's treasure. It also contributes to the color and vibrancy of the neighborhood through its ArtUp project—painting murals on city scaffolding, Dumpsters, sidewalks, and streets.

The Puerto Rican Community

The subject of arts and culture would not be complete without mentioning the presence and contributions of the Puerto Rican community in the East Village. As a result of large numbers of migrants arriving in the United States from Puerto Rico starting in the 1950s, the Lower East Side became a center of Puerto Rican art, music, and literature. As a result of the new waves of migrants from the island:

> New terminology began to spring up, and the name *Nuyorican* initially started as a kind of insult towards assimilated Puerto Ricans or second and third generation Puerto Ricans who have lost touch with their island roots. Traditionally, Nuyoricans planted their flags in what became known as "Spanish Harlem" in East Harlem, and "Loisaida" in the East Village, a Nuyorican pronunciation of "Lower East Side." (National Trust for Historic Preservation)

The newcomers from Puerto Rico and their descendants have effectively stood up to forces within the larger society that worked to marginalize them, and those in the Puerto Rican community have joined together to stake their claim on the New York City neighborhoods in which they live.

One manifestation of this pride and determination of the Puerto Rican community in the East Village is the Loisaida Center on East Ninth Street. Their programs and facilities are extensive and include a media studio and the innovative Media Used for Justice Equity and Respect (M.U.J.E.R) program. Participants apply for the eight-to-twelve-week program and "applications are reviewed by a committee of fellow artists, professionals, educators, counselors, and community leaders" (Loisaida Center). The center also has an artist residency program and, for more than thirty years, has sponsored the annual Loisaida Festival, the largest community pride festival in the neighborhood, one that attracts over 25,000 attendees every year.

CONCLUSION

There are many more community organizations in the East Village and on the Lower East Side than are presented here. There are public, private, and faith-based organizations that provide meals and food pantries, shelter, job-search assistance, as well as a wide range of other services for children, families, and seniors.[4] Community gardens have been nurtured there over the years, including the Loisaida United Community Gardens (LUNGS), providing peaceful green spaces amid the concrete and busy thoroughfares. Together, these different initiatives, groups, and places have addressed the needs of their neighbors, working to satisfy the impulse among all of us to live in a clean, safe, and welcoming environment. They also draw on a long history of a community, which, in the face of health and environ-mental crises, economic upheavals, and demographic changes, has nonetheless endured. This has largely been accomplished through the ever-changing community's own determination and agency, but also taking into account that "a neighborhood's future is as much the product of unintended consequences as intended ones" (Abu-Lughod 1994, 351).

FINAL THOUGHTS

WHEN I FIRST ENCOUNTERED the letters between Helen Schechter and her Christodora House teacher, the context of their relationship and place in New York City were not clear to me. There are still pieces to their story that may never be recovered, but I have a much better idea of how those two women came together and what their role in settlement house and New York City house history was. I have walked through the doors of Christodora House, sat in Tompkins Square Park, pored through the material in archival collections and libraries, and corresponded with a variety of people who work in current settlement and community houses. In addition, I have spoken in person and by phone with individuals who have worked for decades with young people at summer camps and after-school clubs, as well as individuals who tirelessly advocate for the programs of Christodora, an organization that still bears the name of the original settlement house on Avenue B. And that just scratches the surface of the interactions I have had and the information I have gathered on this project.

This is what I have learned. Our cities and the people in them are precious resources, but they have not always been cared for and appreciated to the degree they deserve to be. Jane Addams's hope that settlement houses might someday not be necessary was naïve in the sense that she believed that city residents and lawmakers and businesses were fully capable of working in harmony together and for social justice and that they would carry through with it. But her vision, the same one that Lillian Wald and Christina MacColl and Jacob Riis and countless others held in their heads and hearts, refuses to go away. There are now, and will always be, individuals and groups of people who listen to others and who respond to the current needs of those human beings who are either like or very different from themselves. They work in cooperative structures like settlement houses, and these dedicated people do not stop there; they also anticipate future crises and problems. There will also always be organizations that value creativity and beauty and expression and the incredible growth that children, teenagers, and adults are capable of. There are educators who work in schools and educators who do not even call themselves teachers but who are nonetheless. And there are places like the East Village, Chinatown, East Harlem, and Mott Haven where young and old work together to make sure there are safe places to gather and study, receive a hot meal, or get help filling out a job application form. These places also, whether in the middle of everyday struggles or in the face of a health or economic crisis, are full of caring, thoughtful people, young and old, who, every day, illustrate the ways in which care for one another, resistance, and resilience live on.

I close with the poem by Margaret Widdemer that, to me, illustrates how joy can be found just about anywhere, and when you do find it, it needs to be cherished.

Dancers (n.d.)
Margaret Widdemer

I saw a beautiful thing last night—
Tired women dancing underneath a light,
Hand on hip, indomitable, gay,
After the day's work they danced the night away.

Each had known sorrow, each had known grief,
But she leaped up and down like a twirling leaf;
Life had done to each of them all Life can do,
But she sprang and twinkle-footed all the night
through;

Scarlet bodice and gay bound head,
Flying petticoats of yellow and red,
Shouting and springing and panting for breath
As if there were no sorrow, as if there were
no death.

Life kept no joy for them and no surprise,
But they sang and danced because their hearts
were wise—
They had learned from love and pain and all
the rest
That out of all living, brave laughter is the best—

I saw a beautiful thing last night—

Tired women dancing underneath a light.

Figure C.1. Christodora Settlement House opposite Tompkins Square Park, Avenue B, New York City. Photo 1929, by Irving Underhill (1872–1960), Museum of the City of New York.

ACKNOWLEDGMENTS

I OFTEN READ OTHER authors' acknowledgments and realize how important it is to show gratitude when you have the chance. There are many people I want to thank for helping me get the project off the ground, gather material for the book, and finally see it through to completion.

First of all, I appreciate the work of all librarians and archivists, especially those at the New-York Historical Society and Columbia University's Rare Book and Manuscript Library in New York City. Tammy Kiter, formerly at NYHS, was especially valuable in assisting me at the very beginning. I also would like to thank the librarians at the University of Northern Iowa in Cedar Falls and Jim O'Loughlin, Julie Husband, and Jake Volk in the Department of Languages and Literatures, who provided assistance and encouragement these past months.

A special thank you to Laura Sewell and Hew Evans at the East Village Community Coalition (EVCC), and Richard Moses, Deborah Wye, and Laura (again) at the Lower East Side Preservation Initiative (LESPI). The Writers' Colony at Dairy Hollow, in Arkansas, was a peaceful place to work and hobnob with other writers like Kelly Anderson. The directors, board members, and Jana Jones at the Writers' Colony have also been very supportive over the years.

At the Christodora organization, I have Ted Elliman, Pamy Manice, Judy Rivkin, Julie Dauer, and Alexis Agliano Sanborn to thank. At University Settlement, Melissa Aase generously agreed to be interviewed at a moment's notice, and I learned so much from her about the oldest settlement house in the United States. Lynne Elizabeth at New Village Press had confidence in me and supplied a great definition of community building: "the human motivations and nitty-gritty work for making a certain part of the world a better place."

Friends Kris Knebel, Cheryl Roberts, Lena Alm-Stävlid, Dominique Winders, Benjamin Hudson, and Elzbieta Black were there when I needed them, as, of course, were my husband, Joseph; dog, Tilda; and siblings Janet and Len and their families. I am also grateful for the many strangers in Iowa, New York, Arkansas, Wisconsin, and Illinois who helped me practice my ever-evolving elevator pitch for this book and who patiently listened and asked questions about settlement houses and Christodora House in particular.

Finally, to those who worked in the past and still perform their magic at settlement houses, schools, nonprofits, and social service organizations: You are always thinking of others first and the world would be a better place if there were more among us who followed your lead.

NOTES

CHAPTER 1

1. An editorial in a Virginia newspaper as early as 1874 contained the phrase "We are a nation of immigrants," predating Kennedy by more than eighty years.

2. Many Jewish immigrants who are now described as Polish were recorded as coming from Russia or other political entities that may no longer exist. Helen Schechter, the writer of the letters that prompted this book, emigrated from Galicia, a region that was once a part of the Austro-Hungarian Empire. In present-day Europe, the region of Galicia is divided between Western Ukraine and Eastern Poland.

CHAPTER 2

1. Even though Riis's work was popular at the time it was written, the reader of today may be shocked by how the writer refers to the people for whom he had sympathy. About Jews, he said, "Money is their God," and on Chinatown: "Stealth and secretiveness are as much part of the Chinaman in New York as the cat-like tread of his felt shoes." It could be said that Riis was only playing to his audience, but it is sad that such characterizations endure alongside his poignant depictions of immigrants as "heroic men and women striving patiently against fearful odds."

2. Ida Tarbell preferred to be known as an historian rather than muck-raker, and Theodore Roosevelt sent health inspectors to meat-packing plants after meeting Upton Sinclair in person.
3. Club women were also known to take on the role of reformer, jour-nalist, or union organizer (or a combination of these) at different points in their lives and careers, depending on where they lived and who was in their social or professional circles.

Chapter 3

1. Vida Scudder struggled to reconcile her religious and political lean-ings in her personal and academic lives. Even though a number of parents whose daughters attended Wellesley College complained about Scudder's socialist activities, she was able to remain on the Wellesley faculty and continued to be politically active.
2. The distribution of a portion of the James fortune to Christo-dora House and other charities was the subject of a protracted legal battle between the charitable organizations and the James Foundation Trustees. This will be described in more detail in chapter 5.
3. Bernard Warach wrote a letter in 1965 to Christodora House in which he let its director know that the Emmanu-El Midtown YM-YMHA building then on East Sixth Street would be soon be avail-able to purchase. It is a testament to Warach's affection and respect for Christodora that he kept in touch with the organization in adulthood and in his capacity as a social work professional.

Chapter 4

1. June Hopkins, granddaughter of Harry Hopkins, wrote several books and articles about her grandparents' lives, and I refer to her work throughout this book.
2. Universities were often associated with settlement houses and the houses' names often reflected this link to either colleges or univer-sities in general or a local institution of higher learning. Examples include University Settlement and College Settlement, of which there were several throughout the country, including in New York and Pennsylvania.

3. In one of the letters Helen Schechter wrote to Ellen Gould, Schechter related how one of her young sons had been given an adult library card by mistake. Incensed, Schechter made sure that this error was corrected and that her son had access only to children's books from then on.
4. Some sources date the start of the Poets' Guild as 1919, but the records I have seen date its first year as 1920.
5. There are different accounts of what happened when the city of New York took over the building at 143 Avenue B, including that it was wrongfully "condemned." The accounts I have consulted reported that the city exercised the power of eminent domain, which involves taking over property for public use and paying the original owner "just compensation" in exchange. There is evidence that there was negotiation over how much the building was worth, but it is unclear whether Christodora contested the takeover altogether. The legal process and procedure of eminent domain is also, confusingly, referred to as "condemnation."

Chapter 5

1. Even though Christodora bought two buildings on First Street, the location is often referred to in the singular.
2. The office on West Twelfth Street was reported to have been used for the employment programs in 1969–1970 and may have operated there in other years as well.

Chapter 7

1. I contacted the author of this article by email on October 20, 2022, and asked him about the meaning of the term *social lift* in this context. This is his explanation.
2. Henry Booth House was founded in 1898, the same year the Young Women's Settlement became Christodora House. Hull House had come into being nine years earlier, in 1889.
3. Mutual trust was especially important in the development of public health nursing and in the Visiting Nurse Service that emerged from the work at the Henry Street Settlement established by Lillian Wald and Mary Brewster on the Lower East Side in 1893.

CHAPTER 8

1. Julia Lathrop, one of the Hull House activists and a participating researcher in the study, disliked the label "slum" for the settlement's Chicago neighborhood. She wanted to make a distinction between the conditions of the neighborhood and the people who lived there, and she characterized local residents as not so different from those who lived in better circumstances.

2. The name "settlement" or "settlement house" was often an issue because, with time, people had not understood what the term meant or what the underlying history was. Some settlement houses changed their names to "community house" or something similar, while others held on to the settlement house name as a badge of honor and a direct line to the past.

CHAPTER 9

1. There had been a permanent band shell in the park in previous years, but the city of New York tore it down in 1991 following yet another protest about the homeless in the park. As of 2022, the band shell had not been rebuilt.

2. The sixteen-story Christodora House building, built in 1928, was considered remarkable when it was first constructed and still stands much taller than the surrounding buildings. The architect, Henry Pelton (1867–1935), was known for designing majestic buildings that soar over adjacent structures, the most well known of which is Riverside Church on the Upper West Side of Manhattan.

3. These figures are for the Chinatown/ Lower East Side PUMA (Public Use Microdata Area). The median property value in 2020 in this part of Manhattan was three times the national average.

4. Many of the same qualities are also characteristic of organizations in the Chinatown area, which together with the Lower East Side, the East Village, and Two Bridges make up Manhattan Community District 3.

BIBLIOGRAPHY

Abu-Lughod, Janet. 1994. "The Battle for Tompkins Square Park." In *From Urban Village to East Village*, 233–66. Cambridge, MA: Blackwell, 1994.

———. 1994. "Welcome to the Neighborhood." In *From Urban Village to East Village*, 17–40. Cambridge, MA: Blackwell, 1994.

Addams, Jane. 1902. *Democracy and Social Ethics*. London: Macmillan Press.

———. 1910. *Twenty Years at Hull-House*. New York: Macmillan.

Anbinder, Tyler. 2016. *City of Dreams*. Boston: Houghton Mifflin Harcourt.

Avenues for Justice. https://www.avenuesforjustice.org.

Bagchee, Nandini. 2018. *Counter Institution: Activist Estates of the Lower East Side*. New York: Fordham University Press.

Batlan, Felice. 2005. "Law and the Social Fabric of the Everyday: The Settlement Houses, Sociological Jurisprudence and the Gendering of Urban Legal Culture." *Southern California Interdisciplinary Law Journal* 15 (2): 235–85.

Battilani, Patrizia, and Harm Schröter. 2012. *The Cooperative Business Movement, 1950 to the Present*. New York: Cambridge University Press.

Bender, Thomas. 2008. "Perils of Degeneration: Reform, the Savage Immigrant, and the Survival of the Unfit." *Journal of Social History* 42 (Fall): 5–29.

Binder, Frederick, David Reimers, and Robert Snyder. 2019. *All the Nations Under Heaven*. New York: Columbia University Press.

Blackwelder, Julia. 1997. *Now Hiring: The Feminization of Work in the United States, 1900–1995*. College Station: Texas A & M University Press.

Blunt, Alison. 2008. "The 'Skyscraper Settlement': Home and Residence at Christodora House." *Environment and Planning* 40 (3): 550–71. DOI:10.1068/a3976.

Bocanegra, Michelle. 2002. "Surging NYC Rents Are Displacing Tenants Who Got Discounts Early in the Pandemic, Report Says." *Gothamist* (July 26). https://gothamist.com.

Bucks County Artists Database. https://www.michenerartmuseum.org.

Carnegie, Andrew. 1906 [1889]. "The Gospel of Wealth." *North American Review* 183 (September 21): 526–37.

Carson, Mina. 1990. *Settlement Folk: Social Thought and the American Settlement Movement, 1885–1930*. Chicago: University of Chicago Press.

Center for Jewish History. "Records of the Industrial Removal Office." https://archives.cjh.org.

Childers, Jay. 2015. "Defining the Right Sort of Immigrant, Theodore Roosevelt and American Character." In *The Rhetorics of U.S. Immigration: Identity, Community, Otherness*, ed. E. Johanna Hartelius, 183–203. University Park, PA: Pennsylvania State University Press.

Christodora House Collection. 1902. "Christodora House Annual Report 1901–1902." Rare Book and Manuscript Library, Columbia University, New York, NY.

———.1908. "Constitution of Christodora House, Article II."

———. 1914. "Christodora Annual Report, 1913–1914."

———. 1915. "Christodora House Yearbook."

———. 1917. "Christodora House Northover Camp Report."

———. 1922. "Christodora House: Informational Brochure."

———. 1927. "Christodora House Board Meeting."

———. 1930. "Christodora House Constitution, Article II."

———. 1933. "Christodora House Facilities and Activities."

———. 1933. "History of Christodora House as Told by C. I. MacColl to a Group of Residents on November 19."

———. 1935. "Christodora House Annual Report 1934–1935."

———. 1939. "Memorial to Christina MacColl."

———. 1940. "Letter from William Krampner."

———. 1941. "Notes on the History of Christodora House."

———. 1942. "Christodora House Annual Report 1941–1942."

———. 1947. "Letter from Herbert Biele to the Board of Directors."

———. 1949. "Christodora House Annual Report 1948–1949."

———. 1950. "Christodora House Annual Report 1949–1950."

———. 1952. "Christodora House Annual Report 1951–1952."

———. 1954. "Christodora House Annual Report 1953–1954."

———. 1956. "Christodora House Annual Report 1955–1956."

———. 1962. "Memo from Stephen Slobadin to Frederic Lincoln," January 2.

Christodora Inc. n.d. "Programs." christodora.org.

———. 1986. "The Christodora Foundation: Its Emerging Role in Filling the Need for Science, Natural History, and Environmental Education Within Urban Communities."

———. 2006. "Christodora Inc. Annual Report."

———. 2021. "Christodora Gala 2021, Sin Senh Remarks." https://www.youtube.com/watch?v=8_UBwywN4pI

Cohen, Julie Schumacher. 2020. "America Is a Nation of Immigrants? Not Precisely." *Ignatian* Solidarity Network, *Voices for Justice Blog* (December 12). https://ignatiansolidarity.net/blog/2020/12/02/america-nation-immigrants-not-precisely/.

Crocker, Ruth. 1992. *Social Work and Social Order: The Settlement Movement in Two Industrial Cities, 1889–1930.* Urbana: University of Illinois Press.

Data USA. "Chinatown and Lower East Side Public Use Microdata Area (PUMA) NY." https://datausa.io

Davis, Allen. 1967. *Spearheads for Reform: The Social Settlements and the Progressive Movement, 1890–1914.* New York: Oxford University Press.

Desipio, Louis, and Rodolfo de Garza. 2015. *U.S. Immigration in the Twenty-First Century: Making Americans, Remaking America.* New York: Taylor & Francis.

Dunbar-Ortiz, Roxanne. 2021. *Not "A Nation of Immigrants:" Settler Colonialism, White Supremacy, and a History of Erasure and Exclusion.* Boston: Beacon Press.

Ellman, Abigail, Juan Rivero, Laura Sewell, and Lily Zaballos (2022). "Crisis and Adaptation: Storefront Trends in the East Village, 2019–2021." https://coopersquare.org

Faderman, Lillian. 1981. *Surpassing the Love of Men: Romantic Friendship and Love Between Women from the Renaissance to the Present.* New York: William Morrow.

———. 1999. "Surpassing the Love of Men Revisited." *Harvard Gay and Lesbian Review* 6 (Spring): 26.

Ferré-Sadurní, Luis. 2018. "The Rise and Fall of New York Public Housing: An Oral History." *New York Times* (July 9).

Fisher, Robert, and Michael Fabricant. 2002. "From Henry Street to Contracted Services: Financing the Settlement House." *Journal of Sociology and Social Welfare* 29 (September): 3–27.

Flynn, Sean. 2019. "Elusive Millionaire Comes Alive in New Book." *Newport Daily News* (May 17). heraldnews.com.

Gendzel, Glenn. 2011. "What the Progressives Had in Common." *The Journal of the Gilded Age and Progressive Era* 103: 331–39. https://doi.org/10.1017/S1537781411000089.

General Federation of Women's C https://www.gfwc.org

Giunta, Edvige, and Mary Anne Trasciatti, eds. 2022. *Talking to the Girls: Intimate and Political Essays on the Triangle Shirtwaist Factory Fire.* New York: New Village Press.

Glazier, Jack. 2006. *Dispersing the Ghetto: The Relocation of Jewish Immigrants Across America.* East Lansing: Michigan State University.

Goldman, Emma. 1931. *Living My Life.* New York: Alfred A. Knopf.

GOLES (Good Old Lower East Side). https://www.goles.org

Gordon, Janet. 1994. "A Resident's View of Conflict on Tompkins Square Park." In *From Urban Village to East Village,* ed. Janet Abu-Lughod, 217–31. Cambridge, MA: Blackwell.

Gregory, James. 2005. *The Southern Diaspora: How the Great Migrations of Black and White Southerners Transformed America.* Chapel Hill: University of North Carolina Press.

Gruenewald, David, and Gregory Smith, eds. 2008. *Place-Based Education in the Global Age.* London: Routledge.

Halpern, Robert. 1995. *Rebuilding the Inner City: A History of Neighborhood Initiatives to Address Poverty in the United States.* New York: Columbia University Press.

Hamilton-Madison House. http://www.hamilton-madisonhouse.org

Hansan, John. 2011. "Settlement Houses: An Introduction." Virginia Commonwealth University, Social Welfare History Project. https://socialwelfare.library.vcu.edu

Helen Schechter Letters. 1918 and undated. MS 2958.8679, New-York Historical Society Manuscript Collections.

Henry Street Settlement. https://www.henrystreet.org.

Hopkins, June. n.d. "Harry L. Hopkins (1890–1946)—Social Worker, Architect of the New Deal, Public Administrator and Confidant of President Franklin D. Roosevelt." Virginia Commonwealth University, Social Welfare History Project. https://socialwelfare.library.vcu.edu.

———. 1999. *Harry Hopkins: Sudden Hero, Brash Reformer.* New York: St. Martin's Press.

———. 2011. Christina Isobell MacColl (December 1864–1939): Founder of Christodora House on the Lower East Side of New York. Virginia Commonwealth University, Social Welfare History Project. https://socialwelfare.library.vcu.edu.

Hounmenou, Charles. 2012. "Black Settlement Houses and Oppositional Consciousness." Journal of Black Studies 4 (September): 646–66.

Jacob Lawrence Migration Series. https://lawrencemigration.phillips collection.org.

James, Cathy. 2001. "Reforming Reform: Toronto's Settlement House Movement, 1900–1920." *The Canadian Historical Review* 82 (1): 55–90.

Johnson, Geoffrey. 2010. "The True Story of the Deadly Encounter at Fort Dearborn." *Chicago Magazine* (January 4). https://www.chi cagomag.com.

King, Michelle. 2011. "Working with/in the Archives." In *Research Methods for History*, ed. Simon Gunn and Lucy Faire, 13–29. Edinburgh: Edinburgh University Press.

Klapper, Melissa. 2005. *Jewish Girls Coming of Age in America, 1860–1920.* New York: New York University Press.

Kraus, Harry. 1980. *The Settlement House Movement in New York City, 1886–1914.* New York: Arno Press.

Lengermann, Patricia, and Jill Niebrugge-Brantley. 2002. "Back to the Future: Settlement Sociology, 1885–1930." *American Sociologist* 33 (1): 5–20.

Lerner, Gerda. 1974. "Early Community Work of Black Women." *The Journal of Negro History* 59 (2): 158–67.

Lin, Jan Chien. 1994. "The Changing Economy of the Lower East Side." In *From Urban Village to East Village*, ed. Janet Abu-Lughod. Cambridge, MA: Blackwell.

MacColl, Christina. 1903. Letter to Josephine Sewall (May 18). Christodora House Collection, Rare Book and Manuscript Library, Columbia University, New York, NY.

———.1908. Letter to unknown recipient. Christodora House Collection, Rare Book and Manuscript Library, Columbia University, New York, NY.

Maffi, Mario. 1995. *Gateway to the Promised Land: Ethnic Cultures in New York's Lower East Side.* New York: New York University Press.

McDermott-Murphy, Caitlin. 2022. Women in STEM Need More Than a Law. *The Harvard Gazette* (June 22). https://news.harvard .edu/gazette.

McGerr, Michael. 2003. *A Fierce Discontent: The Rise and Fall of the Progressive Movement in America, 1870–1920.* New York: Free Press.

Meacham, Jon. 2018. *The Soul of America: The Battle for Our Better Angels.* New York: Random House.

Mele, Christopher. 2000. *Selling the Lower East Side: Culture, Real Estate, and Resistance in New York City.* Minneapolis: University of Minnesota Press.

Mooney, Jake. 2008. "The Yuppie Scum Weigh in, Twenty Years Later." *New York Times* (August 8).

Moore, Deborah Dash, Jeffrey Gurock, Annie Polland, Howard Rock, Daniel Soyer, and Diana Linden. 2017. *Jewish New York: The Remarkable Story of a City and Its People.* New York: New York University Press.

Muncy, Robyn. 2006. *Creating a Female Dominion in American Reform, 1890–1935.* Oxford: Oxford University Press.

Nadel, Meryl, and Susan Scher. 2022. "Linkages: Settlement Houses, Summer Camps, and the Origins of Social Group Work." *Social Work with Groups.* DOI: 10.1080/01609513.2022.2113250.

National Trust for Historic Preservation. https://savingplaces.org.

New-York Historical Society. https://www.nyhistory.org.

New York Times. 1934. "First CWA School Picked." *New York Times* (January 16).

———. 1938. "YMCA Wins Tax Suit; High Court Exempts Sloane House and
Christodora House." *New York Times* (July 9).

———. 1947. "City to Get Settlement" *New York Times* (October 31).

———. 1950. "Settlements Help Housing Projects." *New York Times* (February 6).

Nigro, Carmen. 2018. Tenement Homes: The Outsized Legacy of New York's Notoriously Cramped Apartments. *New York Public Library Blog* (June 7). https://www.nypl.org/blog/2018/06/07/tenement -homes-new-york-history-cramped-apartments.

Nugent, W. (2010). *Progressivism: A Very Short History.* New York: Oxford University Press.

NYC-Arts. https://www.nyc-arts.org.

Payton, Robert, nd Michael Moody. 2008. *Understanding Philan- thropy: Its Meaning and Mission.* Bloomington: Indiana Univer- sity Press.

Plunz, Richard. 2016. *A History of Housing in New York City.* New York: Columbia University Press.

Polland, Annie, and Daniel Soyer. 2012. *Emerging Metropolis: New York Jews in the Age of Immigration, 1840–1920.* New York: NYU Press.

Price, Todd. 2011. "Kingsley House: Improving Life in the City for 100 Years." *New Orleans Living Magazine* (October 4). https://www .livingneworleans.com.

Purdum, Todd. 1988. "Melee in Tompkins Square Park: Violence and Its Provocation." *New York Times* (August 14).

Reaven, Marci, and Jean Houck. 1994. "A History of Tompkins Square Park." In *From Urban Village to East Village,* ed. Janet Abu-Lughod, 81–98. Cambridge, MA: Blackwell.

Rees, Jonathan. 1997. "Homestead in Context: Andrew Carnegie and the Decline of the Amalgamated Association of Iron and Steel Workers." *Pennsylvania History: A Journal of Mid-Atlantic Studies* 64 (Autumn): 509–33.

Reinders, Robert. 1982. "Toynbee Hall and the American Settlement Movement." *Social Service Review* 56 (1): 39–54.

Reppy, Dorothy, and Karen Larwin. 2019. "The Association Between Perception of Caring and Intrinsic Motivation: A Study of Urban Middle School Students." *Journal of Education* 200 (1): 48–61. doi .org/10.1177/0022057419875123.

Residents of Hull-House 2007 [1895]. *Hull-House Maps and Papers.* Urbana: University of Illinois Press.

Riis, Jacob. 1997 [1890]. *How the Other Half Lives.* New York: Penguin Classics.

Roosevelt, Theodore. 1906. "Address of President Roosevelt at the Laying of the Cornerstone of the Building of the House of Representatives" (April 14). https://voicesofdemocracy.umd.edu.

Rosen, Miss. 2019. "The Explosive Rise and Inevitable Downfall of the East Village Art Scene." documentjournal.com.

Rubin, Joan. 2007. *Songs of Ourselves: Uses of Poetry in America.* Cambridge: Harvard University Press.

Scott, Emmett J. 1920. *Negro Migration During the War.* New York: Oxford University Press.

Sherwood, Robert. 1948. *Roosevelt and Hopkins: An Intimate History.* New York: Harper & Row.

Siegel, Jefferson. 2022. "East Village's Avenues for Justice Program Honored with Street Co-naming." *The Village Sun* (May 22). https://thevillagesun.com.

Sinclair, Upton. 1906. *The Jungle.* New York: Doubleday.

Sironi, Alice, Céline Bauloz, and Milen Emmanuel, eds. 2019. *International Migration Law: Glossary on Migration.* 34. Geneva: International Organization for Migration (IOM).

Small, Zachary. 2018. "Another Wave of Gentrification Hits the Lower East Side." https://hyperallergic.com.

Smith, Mateo. 2022. "Community Response Team Imprints Itself on the Lower East Side." https://www.henrystreet.org.

Sobel, David. 2004. *Place-Based Education: Connecting Classrooms and Communities.* Great Barrington, MA: Orion Society.

Sofge, Christine. 2004. "To Be of Use: Women of the Settlement House Movement. *History Magazine* (April/May), 22–24.

Soyer, Daniel. 1997. *Jewish Immigrant Associations and American Identity in New York, 1880–1939.* Detroit: Wayne State University Press.

Spain, Daphne. 2001. *How Women Saved the City.* Minneapolis: University of Minnesota Press.

Stebner, Eleanor. 1997. *The Women of Hull House.* Albany: State University of New York Press.

———. 2006. "The Settlement House Movement." In *Encyclopedia of Women and Religion*, ed. Rosemary Skinner Keller and Rosemary Radford Ruether, 1059–68. Bloomington: Indiana University Press.

Steffens, Lincoln. 1904. *The Shame of the Cities*. New York: McClure Phillips.

Steiner, Edward. 1939. "Eulogy for Christina MacColl." Christodora House Collection, Rare Book and Manuscript Library, Columbia University, New York, NY.

Stivers, Camilla. 1991. "Toward a Feminist Perspective in Public Administration Theory. *Women in Politics* 10 (4): 49–65. DOI: 10.1300/J014v10n04_03.

———. 2000. *Bureau Men, Settlement Women*. Lawrence: University of Kansas Press.

Tarbell, Ida. 1939. *All in the Day's Work*. New York: MacMillan Company.

Trolander, Judith. 1975. *Settlement Houses and the Great Depression*. Detroit: Wayne State University.

United Neighborhood Houses of New York. "What is a Settlement House?" https://www.unhny.org.

University Settlement Society (n.d.). "Our History." https://www.universitysettlement.org.

Vaughan, Roger. 2017. *Of Rails and Sails*. Documentary, directed by Joseph E. Daniel.

———. 2019. *Arthur Curtiss James: Unsung Titan of the Gilded Age*. Sonoma, CA: Story Arts Media.

Wald, Lillian. 1915. *The House on Henry Street*. New York: Henry Holt and Company.

Wallace, Mike. 2017. *Greater Gotham: A History of New York City from 1898 to 1919*. New York: Oxford University Press.

Warach, Bernard. 2011. *Hope: A Memoir*. Bloomington, IN: iUniverse.

Weissman, Harold, and Henry Heifetz. 1968. "Changing Program Emphases of Settlement Houses." *Social Work* 13 (4): 40–49.

Whitfield, Stephen. 2013. "Out of Anarchism and into the Academy: The Many Lives of Frank Tannenbaum." *Journal for the Study of Radicalism* 7 (2): 93–121.

Widdemer, Margaret. n.d. "Dancers." Christodora House Collection, Rare Book and Manuscript Library, Columbia University, New York, NY.

Woods, Robert, and Albert Kennedy. 1911. *The Handbook of Settlements*. New York: Sage Foundation.

———. 1922. *The Settlement Horizon: A National Estimate*. New York: Russell Sage Foundation.

Woyshner, Christine. 2002. "Political History as Women's History: Toward a More Inclusive Curriculum." *Theory and Research in Social Education* 30 (3): 354–380.

Wulfson, Myrna. 2001. "The Ethics of Corporate Social Responsibility and Philanthropic Ventures. *Journal of Business Ethics* 29 (1–2): 13–45.

Yee, Shirley. 2011. *An Immigrant Neighborhood: Interethnic and Interracial Encounters in New York Before 1930.* Philadelphia: Temple University Press.

Yochelson, Bonnie, and Daniel Czitrom. 2007. *Rediscovering Jacob Riis: Exposure Journalism and Photography in Turn-of-the-Century New York.* New York: The New Press.

Yung, Judy, Gordon Chang, and Him Mark Lai. 2006. *Chinese American Voices: From the Gold Rush to the Present.* Berkeley: University of California Press.

INDEX

ABOUT THE AUTHOR

JOYCE MILAMBILING is a writer and educator. She has an M.A. in Scandinavian and a Ph.D. in Linguistics and has enjoyed a career teaching foreign language and ESL teachers in the United States and overseas. She is a lifelong traveler and is fascinated by the complexities of history and cultures. A member of the Berkshire Conference of Women Historians and the New-York Historical Society, her articles have appeared in *Academe, English Teaching Forum,* and *Theory into Practice.*